BEAUTY

in the

STILLNESS

Karin Hadadan

**THOUGHT
CATALOG**
Books

THOUGHTCATALOG.COM

THOUGHT
CATALOG
Books

Copyright © 2023 Karin Hadadan.

All rights reserved. No part of this book may be reproduced or transmitted in any form or any means, electronic or mechanical, without prior written consent and permission from Thought Catalog.

Published by Thought Catalog Books, an imprint of Thought Catalog, a digital magazine owned and operated by The Thought & Expression Co. Inc., an independent media organization founded in 2010 and based in the United States of America. For stocking inquiries, contact stockists@shopcatalog.com.

Produced by Chris Lavergne and Noelle Beams
Art direction and design by KJ Parish
Creative editorial direction by Brianna Wiest
Circulation management by Isidoros Karamitopoulos

thoughtcatalog.com | shopcatalog.com

First Edition, Limited Edition Pressing
Printed in the United States of America.

ISBN 978-1-949759-66-2

TABLE OF CONTENTS

for those who yearn to discover themselves—

may you shed layers that no longer align,
and walk away with more clarity.

On

PRESENCE

STILLNESS

I believe I truly understand life after midnight
When I hear the creaks that my heater makes
Or the footsteps in the hallway
The shifting positions of the sheets
Or the cars driving in the streets
But even the absence of bustle
Makes me understand
How when you listen closely
You can grasp everything you cannot see
Because many of us overlook the ability to listen and notice
There is much more than what our retina displays
There is beauty in the stillness

THEN, NOW, AND WHAT'S TO COME

The life you are currently living is a result of your past. It's a combination of every decision you've made, every place you've been, every thought you've simmered in, every feeling you've digested, and every person you've connected with. But the beauty in our human existence is that at any point in time, we have the ability to change what our moments consist of. If you are dissatisfied with where you are or feel resentment towards your story, you do have the power to shift your circumstances. But it is only up to you—because the future you aspire to experience is a result of *your* now. It is rooted in the decisions *you* make today, the places *you* explore, the thoughts *you* dissect, the feelings *you* absorb, and the people *you* encounter, all in this present moment. The secret to pivoting where you are headed is simple—be where your feet are and match the energetic vibration of the life you seek.

BE HERE FULLY

The mere fact about presence is that our lives happen in the now. So when people come in, when experiences are made, when dreams are brought to fruition, when healing takes place…you want to be there fully. You must enjoy it, live it, and love it to its maximum capacity. Even if it is painful, daunting, lonely, or confusing, the present moment is all you ever have, and you must appreciate the totality of it. But if your mind is elsewhere—if you are dwelling on the past or living in the future—your life will move forward, and you won't even notice the changes that are occurring. In its entirety, those changes are what make life as beautiful as it can be.

EYES OPEN

In order for there to be miracles
You must be present enough
to witness the miracles that are already happening

REALIGNMENT

The biggest changes we see in our lives are rooted in the smallest habits. They're how we spend the first hour of our mornings. They're how we nourish our bodies through food. They're how we speak to ourselves when no one is around. They're in the films we watch, the music we listen to, the content we consume. They're the people we give ourselves access to. The way we move our bodies. Where and how we spend our money. When we shift the little intricacies of our lives—when we reconsider how we leverage our personal doings with the outer world—we will notice grand shifts that will realign us on our paths to greatness.

CONVERSATIONS WITH MYSELF

"What is it that you want?" my mind asks.
"A lot of things," my heart whispers.
"But what is it that you really want, really need?"
my mind questions.
"To be happy…fulfilled…powerful!" my heart exclaims.
"How will you be any of those things?" my mind asks,
noticing that my heart is unsure.
"I don't know," my heart replies.
"But what I do know is that I will never stop until I get there."
"Have control over me," my mind states.
*"And you will see that what you want and need is
within you already."*

THE PEACEMAKER

My mind and my heart
Are at a constant war
With no ceasefire in sight
But my soul
The one who sees the light in the darkest moment
The one that honors every piece of my being
The one that brings me back down to earth, here
That fights with strength and resilience
Will raise the white flag
Allowing both to settle down
To be united as one
And allow me to be free

I AM HERE

Today was a lovely day because all I did was sit still in front of the water with a friend of mine and I watched the sun dance on the river and I listened to the people chattering next to me about their dinner yesterday evening and I watched the old man shake his head as he listened to his music and I overheard a dark-skinned man breathing in and out as he ran around the river path and I felt the sensation of the wind blowing through my hair and I engaged in a wholesome conversation that made me feel enlightened and I didn't question anything that was happening around me and instead I opened my ears and my heart and my mind and allowed the world to continue doing its thing and I took it all in and I think that was what made it so lovely because I didn't expect nor wish anything substantial to happen, the world just happened around me and I noticed all of it, and somehow the collective efforts of the souls surrounding me allowed me to realize that what is significant in this life isn't the grand events but instead the micro intricacies that simultaneously intertwine around us, connecting us as one. It is moments like these I wish I could capture and revisit forever.

GETTING YOUR POWER BACK

Learn how to control your thoughts. Control the words you tell yourself, the reactions you have inside of your mind towards external events, and what you place your attention on. Because it is your inner mental attitude that makes your outside world what it is. The way you think either makes life beautiful or unpleasant. What you tell yourself either makes you feel delighted or disappointed. The things you choose to focus on, good or bad, are what will manifest in your life. Adjust your way of thinking, and your life will transform.

HOW TO LIVE IN THE
HERE AND NOW

Select your thoughts
Be aware
Observe what's around you
Act freely
Charge your soul
Remove expectations
Use your senses fully
Control your mind

HIGHS & LOWS

The contrast of emotions is what makes life vibrant. Happiness is not a standalone feeling; it is a comparative emotion, and it is through our lows that we become aware of our highs. The low points allow us to see things more clearly, make critical decisions that will benefit our future selves, and be informed on where we should lean in and what we should step away from. These lessons expose us to a new path filled with bettering ourselves, helping us select the right people we want in our lives, and giving us the opportunity to choose what sort of life we want to live.

A life devoid of sadness, fear, self-doubt, anxiety, stress, and heartbreak restricts our ability to experience those critical lessons, which in the end, lead to high heights of happiness. The space that we're destined to be.

Feel grateful for the contrast of emotions that life is presenting to you right now. Lean into them. Appreciate them. Understand the value of them. Ultimately, they are what allow you to experience a genuine human experience.

A LETTER TO ME

To my previous self: *Thank you for everything you've done to get me to where I am today. You've taught me great lessons that I will carry with me forever.*

To my current self: *Be where your feet are; you're exactly where you're supposed to be. And keep going; you're doing better than you think.*

To my future self: *I can't wait to be acquainted and meet all of the new parts of you. It brings me comfort and excitement that I will encounter new layers.*

To all of my selves: *Let's unite and continue to embark on this journey together. For without one, I am none.*

WHAT IS MINDFULNESS?

It is the act of being aware by noticing the potentially abrupt negative charge generated by your thoughts, emotions, and body, accepting it has emerged and then making the decision to be in control of it instead of being controlled by it.

STATES OF LIVING

The past says, *learn from me*
The present says, *be with me*
The future says, *be inspired by me*

A REMINDER TO SLOW DOWN

Take a breath. Take your time. Be aware of where you are, how you are, and what you are. Pause the constant need to do something, to be something more, or to achieve another goal. Visualize your dreams but don't let them force you to step away from the present moment. Don't compromise the now in order to get lost in the future. Be where your feet are and simmer all that the world is offering you today.

Whether it's a high, a low, or an in-between, this chapter of your life is meant to be savored. It is meant to be enjoyed and experienced to its fullest potential. It will teach you something, or it'll grant you a gift, but it is only when you are in rapid mode that you tend to miss out on the good stuff. The stuff that makes you who you are or the memories that define your existence. So inhale, exhale, slow down. You still have time.

YOU ARE ENOUGH

The reality is—you don't need to make progress all of the time. When you try to make things happen at every moment, you reduce the space to just live. You prevent yourself from enjoying the present as you're constantly doing things for your future self. The precious moments aren't savored. The experiences aren't whole. The contentment isn't felt. Don't ever stop dreaming and chasing your goals, but allow yourself to also pause. The best thing you can do for yourself is to show up every day, be present and simply exist.

LIFE IS MEANT TO BE ENJOYED
AT EVERY MOMENT

There are periods of our lives where the present moment feels so uncomfortable, so distanced from the ideal lifestyle, and so lonely that we resort to the future to feel excitement. We dream big, think deeply, and visualize what the upcoming moments may hold to experience some sort of the thrill. Or we marinate on the past, feeling nostalgic for a time that once was. But by using the past or future to escape the present, when tomorrow comes, we're reminded that the dark feelings never seem to fully go away.

The harsh reality is that our existence is finite. Tomorrow isn't promised; five years from now may never come to be. All we have is the now, but these precious moments are often overlooked. And as hard as it is to find gratitude for what we already have, we must not disregard the blessings that exist around us. The sounds of nature. The lovely people circling us. The radiant health. The nourishing foods. The magic our bodies hold. The feelings we're able to articulate. The laughs we share.

The irony is that the potential that we are chasing or the experiences we are searching for exist within us—not outside of us. But it is only at the current point in time that we have the ability to tap into these sensations—joy, bliss, success, love, confidence—and bring them into reality. Not tomorrow, not a year from today. Now.

SLOW LIVING

When your days feel empty, your heart feels heavy, your mind trends towards comparison, your body feels restless, and your eyes lose focus, you must take a step back and come back to yourself. It is when you feel the discomfort that it's time to prioritize restoration without any guilt and to free yourself from the obligation to do it all, all the time. Remove the ideology that in order to be adequate, you must be useful and productive. Dismiss any thoughts that make you feel like you're falling behind. Remind yourself that your mere existence is enough as it is. Who you are today and what you have now is more than enough. So choose to rest, choose to slow down, choose to move at a steady pace. Because just like the sun and the moon and the stars, we must give ourselves the time to shine bright, the space to revitalize, and the strength to come home again.

On

HEARTBREAK

UNKNOWN NUMBER

The trouble of this life is that none of us ever really say how we feel. How are we still strangers even through all of this? *I'd imagine our feelings are more similar than we expect. Maybe we should talk about them.*

AND AT ONCE, I KNEW
I WAS NOT MAGNIFICENT

When I started to believe in the false narrative I told my friends about him, I noticed my true self disappearing into the void, and there emerged a broken girl who didn't feel worthy enough to not settle.

She was a stranger to me.

YOU EITHER WANT ME OR YOU DON'T

The feeling of my lips pressed against your bare skin, kick-starting the process of little bumps spreading throughout, giving you a sensation that either lingers for days after or perhaps it quickly fades, like a passing thought.

You either crave my voice saying words you've never heard and are mesmerized by how my mind can form sentences so powerful while being made up of the same letters that are used in your name, or perhaps the way my lips move and the things I say have no meaning in your life, just another thing you heard while walking down the street—nothing worth jotting down.

The way I walk into a room can either make your eyes light up brighter than a neon sign on top of a 24-hour convenience store in the middle of a quiet city, or perhaps me coming a step closer to you is nothing but a shorter distance that makes you want to take a few steps back, makes you want to go to your past life with her.

My body next to yours should feel like the home you never had, the safe haven your 13-year-old self needed, the church where all of your prayers will be heard, and the movie screen where you can watch all of your favorite dreams. Or perhaps it is just a figure, another that fits against yours and can satisfy your needs, a mediocre experience that shows how you have control and power over at least one aspect of your life.

The thought of me is either the most mesmerizing particle in your mind, one that consumes all other particles, one that has no weight, nor depth, nor height but feels bigger than anything you've ever seen. Or maybe the image of me in your mind is only seen in the darkest hours of the day, never seeing the light, never fully coming into what could be.

OR MAYBE THERE'S A SEQUEL

For the past few months I have tried to swallow every deep
emotion and feeling I have for you
Burying all of the imaginations, words, and sensual experiences
Removing your memory from my mind,
getting rid of the laughs we shared
I thought I was doing myself a favor
That deleting your presence from my life will allow me
to see what it is I truly desire, seek, and deserve
And for a brief period of time
The thought of you was nowhere to be found in my mind
Or if it was, it had a different sentiment
But the moment I hear from you
The second I get an ounce of your attention or affection
Everything rushes back
The exhilaration
The desire
The craving
It all floods within my heart and mind and soul
And I am trying to drain it out
To not allow myself to get back to where I was last summer,
losing myself over you
But I can't help but let my body and mind
do what it is craving to do
Thinking about you
Yearning for you
Wondering if you're doing the same
Questioning whether there really is another chapter for us
Or if I'm just rereading the same book,
expecting a new ending

WORTH

Know your worth,
I tell myself
Yet every time you disappoint me
I can't seem to hide away

Know your worth,
I tell myself
Yet my fingers still press the letters of your name on my
keyboard
The night ending in me sending you words that shouldn't
have even been in my mind
And soon after I accept your faults to receive an ounce of
attention in the future
Yet to you, my being is not important enough

I am always on your mind, but how much space do I occupy?
You miss my lips pressed against yours, but how long are you
willing to wait?

Know your worth,
I remind myself
And slowly I begin to understand
I am not someone to disturb with no true intention
I am not an option in your Rolodex of lovers
I am not an asset that one is lucky to always have in their bag

I am someone who should be prioritized
I am someone who deserves magnetic attraction
I am someone who warrants appreciation

You name still appears everywhere
Your face is all my eyes see, whether open or shut
But slowly, I will know my worth
And learn when to let go

SCREENWRITER

The battle that we face when trying to let go of someone is whether we should listen to our minds or feel what our heart knows to be true. We make excuses. We try to find closure. We overthink. We spiral. But the art of letting go is not choosing between the mind and heart, it's leveraging both by choosing to surrender. It's feeling compassion for what your mind wants and what your heart knows to be right. It's coming to terms with the fact that the person you're trying to distance yourself from was merely a supporting role in the chapters of your past life. It's allowing your mind to say, *"They'll always hold a special place within me,"* and your heart replying, *"Indeed, but there is more out there."*

When you surrender, you trust that on the next page in the story of your life, something greater lies for you. And it is one of two things or a combination of both: [1] you return the love you had for them back to yourself, and [2] you are introduced to a new being, one who sees how extraordinary you are and is equally as extraordinary as you.

The key is to succumb to the possibility that someone else is out there for you, but it is only when you flip the page that you'll be acquainted with them. You can either re-read the same page or you can write what comes next.

CHANGING YOUR STORY

The narrative that races through your mind, the one that brings pain and suffering, is simply that—a narrative. It is rooted in a conditioned belief that things won't work out the way you hope, or that you are the product of your circumstances, or that your life is just a repetitive cycle of what's happened in the past. When you're in that headspace, the story you continuously replay in your mind will define everything you experience and everything you are, unless you shift the beliefs that are felt deep within. So how much longer are you going to stand in your own way? How much longer are you going to believe that this is it? It is only when you remove the clinging nature that you can stop giving weight to that story, eventually changing who you are. You cannot control what happened, but you can control how you move through the world and how you respond to what comes up. That is how you evolve your storyline.

THE ART OF DETACHMENT

What we don't realize is that when we let go of someone, we're not just letting them go. We're letting our old selves go, too. Detaching ourselves from the identity that we associated with initially feels daunting, messy, and heavy—it is an act of grieving no one prepared us for—but it is also liberating.

Know that we no longer have to be someone who settles. We no longer need to accept the bare minimum. We no longer have to take in emotional baggage that doesn't serve us. We no longer have to witness false promises. We no longer have to feel let down. We no longer have to unlock our phone several times a day in hopes of receiving an apology. We no longer have to tell our friends, *"Yeah, but it's different this time,"* when in fact, it was not. We no longer have to sit in our tub on a Sunday evening with rivers flowing from our eyelids, where even the blistering hot water doesn't numb the pain.

When we detach from that identity, we will see all that we truly are. When we place our energy on letting go of that old version of ourselves, our grip on them will release too.

WINNER

Even though they broke your heart
They also opened your eyes and cleared your mind
That is a win worth celebrating

DO THE SAME FOR YOURSELF
AS YOU WOULD FOR THEM

If you were able to transform them—someone who was
likely ordinary with no complexity, no depth, no unique-
ness—into someone unfathomably perfect in your mind,
why would you ever believe that you couldn't shift the per-
ception of yourself, too?

KEEPING YOUR HEART OPEN

Despite the many setbacks you will face throughout your lifetime, after almost every low point, something magical happens. A sign is shown. A voice is heard. A window is opened. A new path emerges. Even when your heart is broken, your job is unfulfilling, your environment is unfavorable, or your health is declining, the universe sends you subtle gestures just when you need them the most. Little cues. Slight hints. A gut feeling. These all guide you to where you need to be, what you need to change, and how you will get there. Make your heart available, take hold of your own power, and let the universe do its thing.

On

LONELINESS

THE ABSENCE OF FLESH

I always wondered why I loved the rain
The common admiration was towards
the soothing sounds of droplets
The contact between nature and the earth
But for me, it was different
It was a chance for me to be consistently touched

FREIGHT TRAIN RUNNING THROUGH
THE MIDDLE OF MY HEAD

All I wanted was to be asked the questions I was itching to share my answers to, to be appreciated for who I was beyond my body and to be felt without any physical touch. I simply yearned to be seen.

CROWDED ROOM

I didn't quite get it, really. But I noticed how I felt the loneliest when I was around other people. The best way to describe it is that when I'd be physically alone, I'd have the freedom to attach the source of loneliness to my physical body. *"You're feeling lonely because you're literally physically alone. Obviously you feel this way."* And so I'd dismiss it and blame the lack of flesh around me for causing this recurring feeling. But when I was with others, there was no excuse. No vindication of what this heaviness was stemming from. I'd sit around a table, hear a friend tell a joke, yet not listen to the laughs that follow because I'd be too in my head, pondering about my loneliness and questioning what exact moment that evening did I start feeling this way. Sometimes it was because of the lack of connection between the people I was surrounded by, but more often than not, it occurred when I'd be in a room filled with people I genuinely loved.

Usually, I wouldn't be able to snap out of it—it's like I wanted to stay there. I wanted to feel numb. I wanted to dive further into this sensation because the opposite of loneliness—being seen, felt, heard—terrified me. I feared that my intensity would intimidate others, making them run far away from my soul, leaving me stranded. And so I distanced myself from the world around me before the world had a chance to distance itself from me.

Time and time again, there would be warfare in my head, one side fighting for me to break down my walls and the other wanting to be held and nurtured as I was. Often I find myself laying on my couch on a Friday evening while the cars are honking and the city lights are glimmering and my social feed is exploding. I simmer in isolation because the excuse of the lack of flesh feels safe again, and I'd rather be there than in a room where I'm not fully present. I'm learning to be okay with it. I'm starting to believe that maybe feeling safe in my own space and reconnecting with myself is what will reset my system so that I can access the source of liberation and feel whole again.

SECRET GARDEN

I was a contradiction—I had an imminent desire to know what people thought of me, but I had a destructive pattern of never showing all of my layers.

Why did I care so much about their perception when they have yet to experience me in complete form?

SHE'D PREFER TO WALK ON HER OWN PATH

I think I've come to terms with the fact that there will always be a feeling of incompatibility between me and this world, running through my veins. I don't fit into this world. I don't think I ever did. But then again, did I even want to fit in? That would be a waste of a lifetime. I'd rather do my own thing.

YOUR TIME WILL COME, TOO

No matter how much self-love I grew to have I was reminded frequently that everyone around me had found their person and the conversations with my friends quickly turned from, *"I wonder when we'll meet our husbands"* to *"Don't worry, your time will come too,"* which made me want to run and hide away because I didn't want to intrude on double dates when I'd be sitting in the 5th seat without a hand to hold or no one to look across the table to and make eye contact with and when it came time to go out on a Friday night I felt the need to drink one too many tequila sodas because dancing alone while they all had one another made me feel like I wasn't good enough but deep down I knew I was good enough and I loved the way that I danced and the energy I had but there was always the thought of *"I wonder if anyone will notice me tonight"* instead of just dancing aimlessly and ironically no one came up to me and so I prayed to God and asked him *"when is it my time?"* and he quietly whispered *"when the time is right"* and so I moved forward each day wondering if the time was finally right and I was conflicted between *it'll happen when you least expect it* and *you need to put yourself out there more* but then I'd look down at my phone and I'd see the name of a past fling on my screen and my heart would flutter and for a split second I felt wanted and needed and admired and maybe for that second it was enough but part of me hated how much power his name still held and how my mood changed in that split second but I responded anyways and said *"I miss you too,"* but did I really miss him or did I just miss the feeling of someone's arms around me someone's lips kissing mine someone listening to me as I felt vulnerable but

I engaged anyways just to feel anything remotely close to what the people around me were feeling and for a long period I equated those drunk messages to the conversations my friends were having with their lovers about their futures but it was so different oh how stupid was I to think it was equivalent and it wasn't until the next morning I'd be reminded again that there really was a piece of me missing because when I asked her to hang out she said she already had plans with her lover which made me happy to hear but at the same time I felt empty again because I should have plans like that too and so I found myself laying in my bath with hot water running and I couldn't tell what part of the water was from the faucet and which were from my eyelids but both equally burned and a vision of the younger version of me came to my eyes and I wished I could hug her and tell her *I'm sorry it's taking this long* and she responded back *don't worry, I'm still proud of you* that was the moment I realized that I do love myself and all that I feel and that you can feel happy for others but also sad for yourself simultaneously and that maybe I should just accept that I do feel lonely and then I realized that it's a different type of loneliness when you finally feel whole individually and are ready to share your love yet the presence of a partner seems far from reach but while I was in that bath and tears were running I started repeating to myself what God had whispered and maybe one day soon if I kept repeating it I'd start to believe it because my time was soon I knew that to be true and there will be a 6th seat at the table and it'll be a triple date and I'll look across the table and glance at my lover and we'll go out dancing that evening and my hips will aimlessly sway with no objective in mind and the next morning his name will pop up on my home screen and in the background will be a picture of us with love radiating off our faces and I'll feel an overwhelming amount of bliss knowing that I finally made it and how my prayers have been answered and I too found my person and long baths will no longer be filled with burning tears but instead roses and lavender and I'll laugh at the fact that it really did happen when I least expected it.

ROSE COLORED GLASSES

Sometimes everything that we are searching for is already in front of us. We just have to change the lens in which we see things through.

CURLED UP ON THE COUCH

Allow yourself to just be in solitude, without judgment, without guilt. Unplugging from the world doesn't mean that you are being reclusive, unfriendly or that your progress is interrupted. It is an act of self-love by listening to what your mind and body need in that very moment. Slowing down and merely being with yourself is part of the process of becoming whole again, as it allows you to reflect, realign and rebirth. You must shamelessly give yourself space for it.

FINDING ORDER

Start to honor the chaos
Because it is the only source for your genuine discoveries
And what once felt messy and painful and confusing
Will be what kick-starts your evolution
Towards figuring out where and how
You make contact with the world

THE SAGA OF A SOUL

Sometimes we have to remind ourselves that we're never alone. Not really. Because we are eternally connected to the world around us. The sounds of nature must reassure us that even if there are holes within us, the fresh, crisp air will fill us back up. The laughs we hear across the coffee shop are a reminder that any vibration coming from another has the ability to animate a sensation inside of us. The cars in the streets that either follow the same direction as we're headed in or travel in a different one suggest that we are never deserted on our paths. The person we sit next to on a long-haul flight who sparks a conversation is proof that there is always room for new connections that uniquely touch us. Even when we feel isolated, we are always there for ourselves. We are our own companions and supporters and lovers, leaving no room for physical abandonment and instead endless space for deeper understanding. So how could we ever say that we are lonely? When we sit with ourselves in solitude or across earthly matters, we are reminded that we never really are.

WOMAN IN WHITE

Nothing is more freeing than being in solitude, fully enjoying your own company, feeling at peace with yourself, and thinking, *"I wouldn't want to be anywhere else in the world or with anyone else…aside from this moment, here, with myself."*

On

SELF-LOVE

WALKING SOLO

It is quite simple, really. No matter where you are in the world—whether alone, with friends, in your home, in a foreign country, at the office, with strangers… you will always be with yourself. Make sure that you enjoy your own company. It's the only person you are guaranteed to forever be with.

THE COSMOS INSIDE OF MY MIND

I was purely fascinated by everything that existed around me. I wanted to find meaning in all of it. I wanted to desperately understand why people were the way they were. I was curious as to why things were created. Why people feel pain. How people heal. The different languages that exist. The various cultures that roam. The discoveries being made in outer space. I was like a sponge—constantly taking it all in. I wanted to learn about everything there was to know. But sometimes, I wish I could just see things and not dig into them. To not try to find meaning in everything because sometimes, there is no meaning. Things just are. To just watch and not digest, to hear and not listen, to walk and not wonder.

It's strange. The thing that I love the most about myself—my mind—is the thing that terrifies me the most, too. I never know what else it will come up with or what else it will un-cover. But that is the thrill of it. I am an enigma, even to myself.

BODYWORK

There has always been a constant battle in my mind
Between the sentiment I have toward my body
and my physical disposition
Looking elsewhere to find satisfaction
and comfort in what was given to me
Trying to change the way I look, and force myself
to find peace for what I see in the mirror
But it is when I spend moments with my body
Where I push its boundaries and ignite the strength
that each limb has
It is when I connect my mind to my muscle,
my heart towards the sensations
Where I am able to remove the toxic energy
I have been conditioned to hold
And it is when my body shows the true power,
resilience, and commitment it has
That I am proving what capabilities it holds
And it is in those periodic moments where I learn to
appreciate all that my body can do
And not focus on what its potential is
One day soon, those periodic moments will be infinite
That is the day I will embody the meaning of self-acceptance

LOOKING BEYOND YOUR REFLECTION

Does it ever occur to you, that you are not the reflection in the mirror but the cheerful sound that comes out of your mouth when you laugh or the way your mind expands when you see more than what is actually there or your energetic leg movements when you're dancing alone in your bedroom and the way you open your heart towards those that you love. Why give power to the most deceitful object, one that is only made up of different metals, that only shows a flat reflection of the outside but not the inside?

Because our laughs, mind, energy, and hearts cannot be felt through a reflection. It can only be felt through energetic exchanges and experiences. The moment when we fall in love with ourselves for these reasons will be the moment when we love our true selves. And when we have a sense of our true selves, we begin to attract the right things, people, and circumstances into our lives.

STANDING IN THE MIRROR, SHAKING HANDS

In order to build clarity on who you are, sharpen the perception you have of yourself and feel adoration towards your entire disposition, you must answer this straightforward question: *If you had the chance, would you befriend yourself?* Begin with that. Suddenly, you will gain access to what needs adjusting and what deserves appreciation.

INTRINSIC SELF-WORTH

Promise yourself that you will stop attaching your self-worth to things that exist outside of you. Things like your job, where you live, your achievements, your perceived failures, the opinions of friends, the approval of others, the actions, or lack thereof, from people you love.

Promise yourself that you will realize how these things that exist in your life are only things—external factors that fluctuate throughout the entirety of your life. And when you tie your self-worth to things that fluctuate, the perception of your worth moves up and down, and you begin to give your power to external forces that rule your state of being, allowing them to control your mood and how you feel.

But true self-worth cannot fluctuate, as it isn't a physical thing. Self-worth, when felt from within, pays no attention to external factors. It is a motionless—yet never-ending—feeling of contentment, joy, and satisfaction for all that you are as your current self.

Remove the attachments for things that exist outside of you, and honor the person you are at your core.

MORE THAN ENOUGH

What if we decide to tell ourselves the beautiful words we so passionately tell others, compliment ourselves the way we compliment our closest friends, accept our flaws similar to how we look past those of our peers, or give ourselves a second chance like how we've forgiven others and allowed them to try again?

What if we allowed ourselves to take a break, like the advice we give when our friends are feeling drained. Or we give more power to our positive qualities and less weight to the things we want to change, like how we do when we're in love and decide to dismiss the negative attributes of our lovers? Or if we decide to celebrate our small wins and allow ourselves to feel joy when we've taken a new step, similar to how we do when our friends accomplish something small that they were excited about?

If we love ourselves at the same capacity as we love those around us and treat ourselves equally to the way we treat others, we will all realize—we are more than enough.

BE YOUR OWN CHEERLEADER

Celebrate your small wins, the little moments of growth, the times when you've healed things from your past, or the instances where you felt proud of how far you've come. Because no one else will understand how difficult it was to achieve them or how long they took or what depths and lengths you went through to be where you are. No one else will cheer you on as much as you can or give you the congratulations that you deserve. Celebrate your triumphs because how you feel about yourself on a consistent basis is what you will experience every day in your life. And there is no better moment than now to feel pride, joy, and contentment for all that you are, so that you can invite more success into your world.

RELEASING SELF-JUDGEMENT

There will be periods in your life that you continuously replay in your mind—past experiences that bring discomfort, stress, and anxiety in your present. You question why you acted in a certain way, why you said what you did, why you didn't do more, why you chose to stay versus letting go, or why you didn't push yourself harder.

But instead of questioning why we made certain choices, we should tell ourselves: *"I made the best choice I could have at the time, and I will not compare it with what I would do now. Instead, I will accept it and learn from it so that I can make healthier decisions in the now."*

Accept your past to guide your now.

LOOK INWARDS

The real form of self-love is not just treating yourself to small pleasures. It's sitting uncomfortably with yourself, acknowledging your engrained thoughts and beliefs associated with your past, and working towards overcoming them. It's unpacking years worth of emotional addictions. It's removing yourself from the narrative that your mind and body have created. It's letting go of the story you keep telling yourself.

When you change the perception you have of yourself, a transformation of energy will occur. You'll start to break free from emotional fixations, ultimately experiencing joyful liberation. Positive energy will become available to you to create your desired reality. The other side of your pain, guilt, and trauma lies freedom, courage, and bliss. You'll begin to love, respect, and honor your entire self. You'll undergo the impact of your heart opening.

There's a reason why we emphasize the importance of 'self' love—only the self can provide the utmost love that it needs.

TAKE IT TO A NEW LEVEL

It is not until you strip away all of the external noises and forces—the career, achievements, wealth, appearance, approval of others—that you will come back to yourself. You will never fully love yourself if you rely on others' validation and opinion of you. You will never have a sense of self-worth if you place your value on your job title, possessions or accomplishments. Because those things continuously change. They alter over time. And you can't rely on something that is not fixed to tell you what you're worth. The only thing you can do is rely on yourself—the person who always shows up every day for you is you. Place more weight on your values, beliefs, personality, traits, passions, spirit, kindness, and mindset—the things that are intrinsic to you—and you will heighten the perception you have of yourself.

GOING INTERNALLY

When you have clarity on the inner workings of your be-ing, you are creating space to shift the workings of the world that exists outside of you. By releasing your emotions, you allow yourself to renew into a better you. When you evolve into a better version of yourself, you have an extraordinary opportunity—to live the life you've fantasized about for yourself. Anytime you feel a shift, settle into your new form. Understand yourself further. Enjoy the process of becoming and un-becoming, learning and unlearning. This journey of self-discovery is one that never ends because even at your very last moments, you will encounter new volumes of yourself, or you will let go of certain things that no longer align with the place you are in. Gradually move into it. Allow for it. Honor it. Welcome it. Become it.

THE GARDENER

There were holes in my heart
Until I realized
I can plant a seed myself
And grow gardens within them
I will nourish it through my thoughts
Water it with my kindness
And witness the continuous blooming
Season after season

KEEP TALKING

Sometimes I wish I could tell my mind to quiet down
To stop the chatter
To not overthink
"Just be silent, please"
But that voice is also proof
That if it didn't exist
I wouldn't have leaped
I wouldn't have questioned
I wouldn't have walked away
I wouldn't have grown
I wouldn't have become
who I am today

THE VESSEL

Patience is the vessel
That will take you from confusion to clarity
All that it requires
Is the space for it to move
Without an agenda
Without a timeline
Without control

Be patient with yourself
Your inner turmoil will eventually transform
And it will all make sense

PROJECT YOUR OWN LIGHT

Dismiss the advice that you must give the energy that's being given to you. Because what that implies is that your reaction, your efforts, and your love are determined based on the actions of others. And while there are boundaries to be placed, never stoop low enough where you are at the same level as someone who has hurt you. Instead, use your light. Show them how good a heart can be. Reveal to them that you're one of a kind. Don't lower yourself for the sake of others. Instead, show up as a better version of the you that they've been accustomed to. Show up as someone who is warm, kind, tender, compassionate, loyal, and honest. Even if they don't deserve it, show a reflection of your character instead of theirs. They may never see your worth, but your self-worth will be blooming so that you won't even notice their lack of awareness.

GOLD STAR ON THE FRIDGE

Give yourself the credit you deserve
You are here
You are trying
You are devoted
You have this curiosity to know what lives beneath the pain
That in and of itself is enough
Acknowledge your bravery
Take note of your commitment
And be your own cheerleader

THE UNFINISHED PUZZLE

Someone once told me that I was complex
At first I perceived that as never being fully understood
But then I started to like the idea of it
Of being made of various layers,
layers that others are not familiar with
Of being complicated in its natural form,
a place of beautiful contradictions
Of being intricately fabricated by the power above,
wires crossed and all
There would always live a mixture of madness
and sanity inside of my being
I liked knowing that others may never get it
I liked knowing that I was an unpredictable mystery
Even through my own reflection

HONORING ALL DIMENSIONS

You must make it a habit to simultaneously appreciate where you were, accept where you currently are, and admire where you are going. And you must do so through unconditional love. It is through looking at your past and acknowledging all that you've learned. It's being present in the now and applauding yourself for all of your efforts. It's looking at your future and feeling pride for the dreams you've set for yourself.

It's through collectively taking notes on all of the versions of you that have come and passed, and all of the versions of you that you have yet to meet. It's thinking to yourself: *I am no longer there, and I may not be where I want to be yet, but I will learn something very important because of this current experience, and I will love myself through every moment of it.*

ON THE WAY TO SCHOOL

When I was four years old I was misbehaving in the backseat of my car and so my mother turned around and said, *"If you don't behave, no one will like you,"* and in retrospect it's quite amusing for a parent to say that but my child self responded, *"I don't care if anyone likes me, I like me and that's all that matters"* and hearing my mother tell me that story as I was an adult was fascinating, as though she reaffirmed all that I knew about myself. I will embody that energy forever.

HUMAN TO HUMAN EQUIVALENCES

You might be reading this and thinking to yourself, *how did she articulate things that I am feeling, things I have been unable to explain?* It is because we are all the same—souls experiencing similar experiences in varying degrees and capacities, longing to be understood, itching to feel seen, hoping we are not alone.

These words are proof that we are more alike than we know, and the more we acknowledge that the less we resist staying hidden.

THE WORD YOU NEED TO ADD TO YOUR DICTIONARY

Learn to say no. Not only to others but also to yourself. "It won't work out," your mind quietly states. "You're not good enough," it hauntingly whispers. "Something will go wrong," it repeatedly says. "This won't be any different than the past; the pattern remains," it obsessively expresses. You must observe these thoughts and notice them circling your inner orbit, but instead of latching onto them and feeding them as you normally would, be there with them. Dissect them. Understand them. Talk back to them.

What triggered this?
What makes me think this is true?
Do I have proof?
Why now?
Why would I believe this?

Look at them face to face, and instead of resorting to your old patterns, shift your approach and respond, "No, I am not going to close. I am going to think differently."

No, it will all work out.
No, I am good enough.
No, everything will go as it should.
No, I am capable of breaking a pattern.

The power those two letters hold is immeasurable—because what you do with it can either break you or liberate you. Choose liberation.

YOU ARE NEEDED HERE

There are only 26 letters in the alphabet, yet there are endless words, sentences, feelings, lyrics, emotions, and names they are able to form and equate to. This made me wonder—if 26 letters can offer so much, just imagine how the millions of cells in your body can offer the rest of the world.

There is a purpose to your existence.

FIDELITY

I had all of this unspent love
Ready to be given away
But there was no man out there
Who'd accept my currency
What do I do with all of this?
I'll invest in myself

On

HEALING

A GENTLE REMINDER

If all you can do today is be brave enough to continue on your journey despite the pain, you are doing enough. Take it slow. Be kind to yourself. Maintain your faith. This is all happening for your greater good, and you are closer than you think.

RELEASE THE GRIP

When you step into the path of surrendering, life will present whatever experience is the most helpful for the evolution of your mind, body, and spirit. It may disturb you. It may heal you. It may frustrate you. It may serve you. It may confuse you. It may expand you. Whatever experience it is, it will be the moment where your life changes for your greater good. Allow yourself to release your grip. Be open to what unfolds. It might be the answer to the prayers you've been whispering.

WRITING A NEW SCRIPT

The root of your suffering isn't the pain itself
But instead, the emotions associated with your pain:
The sentiment you have towards your body or your story
The feelings associated with the discomfort and the distress
The beliefs around your healing
The source of your ongoing hardships is
the voice inside of your mind saying
You are weak
You shouldn't be here
Get over it already
You deserve this
While you may not have control of where
that suffering turns up in your body
Whether it's a physical manifestation,
a torment of the heart, or an aching wound
You do have control of the way it lives inside of your mind
You are strong
You are exactly where you need to be
Take your time, healing is ongoing
This is happening for you
Change the dialogue
And you will feel liberated

HEAL-ING

Understand that healing is not linear. It is an upward coil where the starting point is the primary source where all of your detrimental beliefs stem from. It is the foundation that leads to every additional detrimental belief, those that hinder your happiness and prevent you from breaking free from suffering. It is multi-dimensional because there are several roots to your pain and once you pull one out, another seed may become visible to you—one that stemmed from the previous source. It is complex because deep-rooted beliefs and traumas will surface when you finally feel like you're getting better, and it'll make you question your progress, although you know in your heart that it is slightly more whole. It is inconsistent because when you're at a peak, it feels as though your mind is finally clear, but you may find yourself at a valley wondering where it all went wrong again. But more than anything, healing is a never-ending journey. One that we must feel gratitude for because without moving around each layer, how would we ever reach the point of knowing what we want to detach from, who we are, and who we want to be?

DEVOTION

I found myself on the floor of my apartment
Knees hammered into the ground
My palms open, facing up, showing mercy
Please, I begged, *take the pain and heaviness from me*
Please, I cried, *release me from this never-ending suffering*
Please, I whispered, *show me that your presence is with me*
Suddenly, all of the stagnant and painful energy
was pulled out of my soul
And was filled with an overwhelming sensation
of warmth and lightness
Keep going, I whispered, *let me fully surrender*
Even though I felt powerless
I chose to release my grip and control
over how I expected my life to unfold
You take over, I murmured
Show me how good it gets
I trust you
I believe in you
That was when the chains unscrewed
I rose up from the floor
And took my first step towards liberation

THE VARIOUS LAYERS

Our healing journey is often seen as this grand event, where one day our hearts will be lighter, our bodies will feel liberated, and our minds will be freed. We perceive it as this singular milestone where everything will suddenly change, and our lives will transform into what we yearn to experience. And anytime we feel we've made progress yet resort back to our old thought patterns or feel as if we're back to where we started, we feel defeated. In those moments of desperation, we must remind ourselves that healing is a journey that will forever continue to unfold. It is a ladder filled with various levels and layers that will continuously force you to become better, all for your greater good. When you heal the first layer, you will be brought higher than where you started. When healing the second, third or fourth layer, you may feel that you have made no progress at all, that nothing within you has changed, and that you will forever be caught in this continuous loop of suffering. But in reality, you have healed many parts of you, which uncovered more learnings about your inner world. It is when you come across new knowledge about yourself that you will be presented with more layers that may still need exploring. But you are not back to where you started—you are at a higher point on that ladder. When you look down, you must notice how much you've restored. You must take note of how much you have evolved and grown. And when you look up, you must feel inspired to keep going. You must be curious and brave enough to see what else you may uncover. You must push yourself to reach the top because as you continue stepping above each level, you are brought closer to your truest, most pure self. And the view will be worthwhile.

THE FIRE WITHIN

I guess maybe I should be angry
And allow myself to feel the rage
buried inside of my heart and mind
I've been so caught up with trying to be perfect
Trying to see the positive
Trying to keep an ounce of hope
Trying to learn the lesson
Trying to believe that everything happens for a reason
That I forgot how sometimes, I just need
to allow myself to feel the anger
The anger towards that person
The anger towards my circumstances
The anger towards my slow healing
To acknowledge that I am hurt
Or pissed
Or frustrated
Or betrayed
Or stuck or confused or lost or just tired
Because that acknowledgment means I am saying:
*"Dear self, I am allowed to feel outraged. I am allowed to feel
resentment. I am allowed to feel the full capacity of my emotions.
I am allowed to be human."*

NOTICE YOURSELF

A sign that shows that you're on the path towards healing is when you experience something similar to what your past self once did, but your reaction today is different. It may be as simple as handling a situation better than a former version of yourself would have been able to. It may be through the shift in your perspective on low moments and how you've learned to appreciate them. It may be that you no longer have an emotional response to previous triggers and instead have broken your association with them. Take note of those moments. Have conversations with yourself when you realize the work you've been doing is working. Take pride in the fact that your commitment to become better is showing off. Download your learnings. Notice your progress. Honor your growth.

POINT OF VIEW

Healing is not only an act but also an attitude—an attitude of believing in yourself and your prayers, trusting that you are capable of repairing imbalances and becoming whole again, and accepting that this rebirth is a power only you hold within.

THIS IS WHAT WILL KEEP YOU GOING

We do not recognize the lowest moments of our lives until after the fact. Even when you feel utmost desperation and sorrow in the present moment, part of you will question that certainly one day soon, there will be a moment when you are drowning even more. And there may be a day when things are worse than before, but a thought will flow through your mind that you must latch onto. *If I've handled things before, I surely can handle this too.* Because how could you not? There is so much more for you to experience that will provide you greater strength and wisdom to get through it. More places to travel to that will shift your perspective. More people you will meet who will open the door to feelings you've never felt. More films to watch that will stimulate your mind. More words to read that will make you feel seen. More conversations to have that will spark something within your heart. Even when you've reached the lowest moment in your life, you must be hopeful enough to believe that your future will hold even an ounce of more beauty. That ounce, even if it's minimal, will lead to the evolution of your strongest self. *Aren't you excited to meet them?*

CANCEL THE SUBSCRIPTION

Remind yourself to not only feel all emotions but also unsubscribe and detach from the story you're affiliating those feelings with. That is how you move forward.

STEPPING BACK TO MOVE FORWARD

Sometimes, it is important to simply step back from your thoughts and let them float inside of your mind. Sometimes all you need to do to move forward is to acknowledge the dark ideas and observe the hurtful words that you tell yourself or the fabricated claims that you try not to believe. Because it is during the act of being mindful and aware of those moments where you feel the weakest that you will be able to decide that you want to step across them, crush them and move past them. And one day, when you begin having positive thoughts, start acknowledging the beautiful words you tell yourself, and become familiar with your new positive self-perception, you will embody the true meaning of utter strength.

BREAKING PATTERNS AND MOVING ON

Often, when we try to move on from something, we dismiss the emotions and feelings associated with it. We unknowingly build up inner resentment, never fully healing or letting go. We tell ourselves that we've moved on, yet days later, we're back where we started, being reacquainted with the same uneasy emotions from days prior. And we ask ourselves, *"Will this pattern ever break?"*

The cure to attaining freedom from what was is to honor it as it is—fully and wholly—and respond differently than previous times. You need to move above the situation for a brief period of time in order to have a full view of what occurred. See what it showed you. Learn how it changed you. Feel what signs it gave you. Honor your inner transformation and allow yourself to completely feel everything that needs to be felt.

When you balance yourself within and understand the source of your feelings and emotions, you can decide to let them pass, creating space for new experiences, beginnings, and lessons. But it is only when we grieve, reflect, and learn that we can eventually respond differently, smile at our growth, and move onto the next chapter in our lives.

PLEASE DON'T GIVE UP;
THE WORLD NEEDS YOU

I hope your heart feels less heavy today
I hope that you haven't let go of the dreams
your child self once had
I hope the world will be kinder to you
and that you receive more love
I hope that you can look at yourself in the mirror
and feel content with the reflection
I hope you can hear yourself laugh
and understand the power your voice has
I hope you are able to bring down the walls
you've built between you and the world,
and I hope you never have another experience
that forces you to build another one
I hope that your mind is at ease, your body at peace
I hope the world allows you to be more vulnerable
and gives you the courage to say what it is you're feeling
I hope your thoughts are no longer dark and lonely,
but light and liberated
I hope you have the strength to continue on your journey
To try again, to have faith, to stay hopeful
Because you deserve to see
What the next version of you will come to be

SOMEWHERE DOWN THE LINE

Whether through an experience, feeling, emotion, thought or person, something within you will shift. You'll wake up feeling different. You'll see the world with fresh eyes. You'll feel gratitude for your past, joy in your present, and excitement for your future. You'll experience forgiveness and you'll witness devotion. Every stinging, lingering thought or unbreakable pattern will suddenly be freed. No longer will the reveries in your mind replay with a cloud of guilt surfacing above them, and the resentment for the cards you were dealt will soon dissipate. No longer will you wish that things ended differently or that your circumstances didn't belong to you. Somewhere down the line, whether near or far, it'll all begin to make sense. And you'll find comfort in the length of time it took you to get there because of the little revelations you've taken with you. When the time comes, the missing pieces will be found, the ones that didn't fit will be discharged, and the masterpiece that is life will unfold. That's the moment you'll say to yourself with the utmost faith, *"It all happened for my greater good."*

BETTER VERSION OF YOUR YESTERDAY SELF

Never aim to be the best version of yourself, for that implies that there is a limit to your being, a threshold that you must meet, a high point that you will eventually reach. Instead, aim to be a better version of your yesterday self, for that implies there is no limit—your growth is infinite and there will always be a part of you that is still out there to meet.

A REPEATED CONVERSATION

Mind: *You'll never get through this.*
Heart: *But I know I can try.*
Soul: *And it'll be worth it.*
Universe: *Because I will guide you.*
God: *And together, we will get through it.*

FOR EMMA, FOREVER AGO

It was when I could listen to the songs that once broke me—the ones that would play in the background as I laid flat on my bed, almost soulless, staring at my ceiling with numbness—and now feel a sense of relief, that I knew I was healing. It was the simple fact that what was once reinforcing my sadness was now providing me a sense of bliss. It touched my soul then, it touches my soul now. Differently, though. That is the power of the chords—they introduce you to what is dormant inside of your heart and light it back up.

On

LOVE

STILL WRITING ABOUT YOU

I can't tell whether I am in love with you
Or the version of you I've designed in my mind
I reminisce of moments where we spent laying on your bed,
laughing in each others' faces
Or sitting in my kitchen, peeling off layers of ourselves
I think about the words that have poured out of your mouth
The words that felt like laying on warm sand
Comforting, yet seductive
I imagine your laugh, your eyes, your smile, your voice, your
body, your walk and your entire disposition
I remember the way you looked at me,
the way your eyes stared into mine
The gaze you had when I walked into my room

But I also think about the conversations that I've fabricated
The words I wished you'd say
The moments I hoped we got to experience
I'd picture how you'd react when I'd say what's on my mind
How you'd appreciate every word that slips off my tongue
You being mesmerized by the way I think
I'd dream of the things you'd do for me

The places we could go together and how we'd interact
I'd ponder you allowing to me part of your life,
you willing to make me more than a fraction of it

Now here I am
Questioning which version I am falling in love with
Wondering maybe, what if maybe,
both versions are the real you
And I have simply yet to experience the second half
Because these fabrications I've created can only be formed
based on reality and what I know of you thus far, right?

While part of me doesn't believe it
I have an ounce of hope that one day
I can experience the version of you I've created in my mind
And that I'll learn how it was not a creation
But instead was foreshadowing what the future holds

TWIN FLAMES

We find ourselves standing across from each other
Both ready to finally walk through the door
The door that leads to one another
And as we're ready to turn the nob
Unleash the built-up tension
Finally reconnect
Rejoice our souls
The universe, God, whatever
Looks down at both of us
Sees the door being cracked open
And uses their power to forcefully ensure it doesn't
It is slammed in our faces
The knob falls off
We are apart
Close yet far
Maybe it's a sign
That despite it all
Forget the words
The memories
The physical sensations
You and are meant to walk on separate paths
You and I are not meant for one another
Otherwise, that door would've opened
We'd rejoice and enter a new dimension
It would've been easy
It would've been effortless

THE HOLLOW WOMAN

A beautiful woman who is only known as a fantasy
in the minds of men
Only seeing her as a perfect fit in between their hands,
But never a perfect fit for their imperfect self

Viewing her body as a temple, rolling their eyes over her mind
Being good enough to be in bed,
being too little for anything else
Neither platonic nor neutral
Purely romantic, without any of the romance
you see in your favorite films

A woman who craves a man's touch
Lingers on the physical sensations for far too long
Ready to give a man what he craves
Despite knowing the repercussions that follow

A woman who claims she understands her worth
Yet doesn't act in accordance with it
And repeats the same heartbreaking patterns
Because that's all she knows

A woman who thinks about her former 'lover'
A mediocre experience that lasted four months
Yet has taken over two years to get over
Who still searches for his face wherever she goes

A woman who says she's ready
Yet runs away from anything that can be permanent

And settles for the mid-20s man who lacks
self awareness or a sense of maturity
Just to repeat the same old pattern that continuously breaks her

A beautiful body is all they see
Nothing less, nothing more
Her heart is closed off
Her mind overthinks
Her lips tend to slow down
All to hide her authentic being
Because for her entire life
No man has been fascinated by her true disposition
Only what her lips and her legs and her hands can do

A FULLY BOOKED FLIGHT

I wanted to take a walk inside of his mind and take in all of the wonders of his inner world. There was so much to see. So much to absorb. So much to uncover. It would've been the trip of my lifetime.

If only he opened the gates.

THE CASE ON LOVE

I knew I had to walk away when I started noticing that I was changing for him. I was altering who I was at my core so that he would give me a little more. But the irony was that even changing who I was didn't make him love me. And truthfully, I did not want to change nor needed to change, and he knew that too. I loved who I was. I loved what I brought to the table. I loved the energy I had. I loved the way my mind did its thing. I loved the way I saw the world. I loved the way in which I loved. But he made me question who I was. I started losing her, changing her, dismissing her. And worst of all—he never changed alongside me. I foolishly thought that maybe if I adjusted, he would too. But he stayed still. And I moved backward. Where he stood wasn't satisfying me. Where I stood confused me. And who he was without my control wasn't nourishing me; it was depleting me.

That was the moment I found myself in a cold and empty room without anyone or with myself. That was when I knew this wasn't love. Because love should be warm. It should be effortless. It should feel safe. And I should be me, and he should be him, and together we should be us.

That is the simple truth about love—it should allow us to be ourselves.

THE MISSING PIECE

They say that people can only meet you as deeply as they've met themselves, so imagine what this world would look like if we all looked inwards, met our souls, and befriended them. If we walked through this earth with the utmost certainty of who we are, we can be face to face with another soul and have our hearts, minds, and paths be aligned.

Maybe that's all we need to do to build more human connection. Maybe discovering ourselves is all we should strive for because the rest will come naturally.

YOU MIGHT NEED TO HEAR THIS

Be aware of how external forces affect your inner peace.
Notice whether their actions and words raise your vibration
or lower it. Acknowledge what is positively feeding into your
energy and what is negatively impacting it. Only you can con-
trol how you respond to external forces and what your body
and mind do with that information affects who you become.

FROM ACROSS THE TABLE

Even if their love was soon to expire, I'd always look deeply into the relationships of others, think about my past failed experiences, and decide that maybe this wasn't ever in my cards. I witnessed it day in and day out. I knew it was real. I knew it existed. I was envious over what others had, yet I felt immune to that sort of love. But I intensely wanted it. I wanted to know what it was like to be someone's first choice. I wanted to know what it was like to feel unconditional love from someone who physically and mentally stimulated me. I wanted to know what it was like to have that one person you can tell your wildest dreams to or your deepest darkest thoughts within minutes of each other and them listening to all of it. I wanted to experience the sensation of never being able to contain myself simply because of the infinite amount of feelings I'd hold for my partner. I trust that when I find it, our love will not expire.

THE NON-EXISTENT MASTERPIECE

But even when he was finally standing in front of me
I yearned for the version of him that I created in my mind
That was the moment I realized
I was never in love with him after all

The intuition never lies

I'VE COME SO FAR

I was proud of myself when despite feeling empty and craving to fill, I stopped allowing myself to settle. I no longer felt the need to make myself smaller to fit the definition of what others thought was love because I finally unraveled my own meaning of it. I now would much rather wait for someone extraordinary than settle for someone average. This was the awakening that my soul required.

WHEN THE TIME IS RIGHT

One day, you will be acquainted with someone where the love you have for them is matched. They'll allow you to see things differently. They'll care for you. They'll be there for you. They'll show you things you've never seen before, feelings you never knew existed, sensations you thought you were immune to. They'll keep your heart safe, your mind at peace, and your body at ease. They'll say those three words, and you'll never have to question whether they meant it because their actions will match. They'll lift you up when you succeed, carry you when you're tired, and hold you when you're broken. You'll see a reflection of yourself in them and they'll provide the balance that you're desperately seeking.

But in the meantime, you must love yourself wholly. You must be good to your own heart and value all that your complex mind and body do for you. You must break the patterned thoughts that you're not worthy and that your heart will forever be closed due to previous toxic experiences.

So please, stay open and invite people into your world. Because when the time is right, someone magical will walk into your life and you want to be in the right headspace to let them in. And when they do, you'll realize that no past lover, novel, film, or song could ever emulate the same love that you'll share with this person.

LET'S GROW OLD TOGETHER

If you can talk to them about anything, anywhere, anytime, and feel exhilaration throughout it all, you've found someone special worth keeping around.

Make it a habit to let them know.

A SELFLESS HEART

I started falling in love with the idea of making others feel loved. I began looking forward to complimenting my barista. Or smiling at the old man who walked past me. Or texting my friend I was proud of her when she got that job she was stressing over. Or telling my Uber driver to get home safe. Or sending flowers to my mother when her day was feeling heavy. Or going to the event my colleague was organizing even though I didn't feel like it. Or letting my friend borrow a book I hadn't finished yet because I knew she needed to read it. Or deciding to pick up the tab when I went out to lunch with my father. Or sending a link to a Spotify playlist that reminded me of her. Or running errands for my brother when his day was filled with meetings.

If we start there—if we start by removing the notion that we must receive love in order to give love, we collectively will be better. I promise you that. Because the more we all give, the more we all feel altruistic, and once we feel this overwhelming sensation, the more it is returned back to us.

To experience this inner revolution—the one where we break down any barriers or limiting beliefs that prevent us from spreading more kindness, and instead open our hearts to-wards others—the more we revolutionize on a societal basis. Because deep down, all we ever want is to experience the utmost amount of love in the years we are here.

When this happens, we will all heal.

THE COLLECTIVE ELEMENTS

My emotions are from my mother
My mindset is from my father
My wisdom is from my brother
My laugh is from my grandmother
My energy is from my friends
My creativity is from the world
My desires are from my role models
My style is from the various decades
We are all intertwined
All connected
What I love about external elements
Is also what is found within me
We are one
We are love

WHAT LOVE IS

Somebody will meet you for the first time, and their initial thought will be, *"My prayers have been answered."* Be patient for that type of love.

THE ANSWER TO MY OWN PRAYERS

I knew I had a crush when I no longer cared what we were talking about, as long as it gave me an excuse to stare at his lips and then his eyes and then back to his lips. I knew he was someone special when he'd be the first person I'd notice while entering a crowded room. I knew it was the beginning of love when I wanted him to be perfectly himself. I no longer had the desire to have him fit the mold of what I thought was a great man because he inherently already was. It was the first time I wasn't searching for the reflection of myself in him. I wasn't searching for anything. I never had to ask for kindness; it came naturally. I never questioned his words because his actions followed. I never wondered if we'd be on the same page since our visions for life were aligned. I never had to mentally outline what I would say since the conversations flowed. I never had to make a plan because he always took charge. I was merely encapsulated by his entire workings—he was an adventure, and I yearned to experience all of it.

CONSISTENT VIBRATIONS

Love should allow two souls to vibrate together at the same frequency, and it should make us feel reborn—over and over and over again. It should be unconditional, feral, compassionate, all-consuming, selfless, numbing, and warm. But it should also allow us to become and un-become through every encounter, every touch, every conversation, every experience, and every feeling.

WHAT LOVE EQUATES TO

When you happily accept others
For their insecurities
Their faults
Their troubled pasts
Their quirky interests
Their unique traits
And you don't question how they are, who they are
And instead, smile at the thought of their entire nature
That is love

SIGNS OF LOVE

This reminded me of you
I'm going to the grocery store, need anything?
Open your door, I sent you a little gift
Did you get home safe?
I am so proud of you
Let's go somewhere together
I'll be here for you
I'll cook this time
How are you, really?
I think you'll like this song
I have an extra ticket
Good luck today
How can I help?
Wanna watch it together?
I can pick you up
Tell me about your day
Remember when we…
Be ready at eight, I have a surprise
Let's work through this together
I can't imagine life without you

THE ARTIST ABOVE

I made a list about the type of man I wanted to fall in love with
Writing down all of the qualities I am seeking
The way he thinks
The way he shows up in this world
The way in which he loves
The way his energy radiates
The way he treats others
For a while I thought it was impossible
To find someone as extraordinary as
the way I described my future lover
Because how can someone like that exist?
Someone so perfect, so perfect for me
But months later
I looked into the eyes of a man and noticed
that what I had written already existed
I realized that the creation in my mind
had already been created by the power above,
many years before my mind was able to formulate
the ideal disposition I was looking for
God brought him to me at the ideal time,
as the version of myself that was ready
to accept him into my world
I thought it was quite magical
Knowing that it had always been written for me
It taught me to never question anything ever again
Because what is meant for me,
Will find me
And the timing will be right

On

GROWTH

YEARLY GROWTH

As you reflect on the person you have become
The person you have grown into
The person that you now are
Feel grateful for all that you have endured
over the past 365 days
The ups and downs
The moments of fear, heartbreak, confusion, loss,
unhappiness, unhealthiness, loneliness
The moments of joy, contentment, fulfillment,
happiness, independence, confidence, power
Because it was through the rollercoaster of life
It was due to the moments where you were the weakest,
the moments where you felt on top of the world
That made you who you are today
It was between those moments of feeling broken and feeling
complete that you became connected with your inner soul,
that you met new parts of yourself
Someone whose soul is filled with life
Passion
Love
Compassion
Positivity
Depth
You have learned so much about the world
and about yourself in just 365 days
And you have yet to love yourself as much as you do
in this current moment
What a powerful year it has been, with this much growth
To another 365 days

EXPLORATION

And just like that
In between cities, time, and memories
You unknowingly become a different person
Part of you has changed
Pieces of your mind have expanded
Segments of your heart have healed
What you thought was important no longer is
And what you imagine as a joyful life has altered
You ask yourself
How much of this new me will stay?
Where did the parts of me that no longer serve me go?
Your old self was left in your home
Your new self has emerged
And you return as someone new
The person you've been striving to be

FEBRUARY 2ND, 2013

I was thinking too much
So I took out my notes app and poured it all out
Turns out I write so I understand my thoughts
So I understand my feelings
So I understand who I am
And document
who I am becoming

My future self will thank me someday

MORNING PAGES

Take note of your life. Write down your experiences. Jot whatever it is you're feeling. Explain the situation that happened. Not for anyone else—but for you. For your future self. Because one day, when you feel happier, when you feel more at peace, when you feel whole, you'll wonder when it all happened. You'll question what moment things started to change. You'll wonder what experience opened the door to your new mind. You'll ask how you were able to adopt a new mindset.

When you take record of your life and the various versions of you, you're giving yourself the ability to pinpoint when the transformation started to occur. In that moment, you'll realize the level of growth that you've been enduring, and you'll feel proud of how far you've come.

TAKE A DETOUR

At every present moment you have two paths to choose from:
One that leads to growth
Or one that leads to safety
Our ego tells us to stay safe
But we've been on that trail before
Maybe we should try switching paths
And see what happens

Maybe the first step is when everything changes

THE WORDS THAT TOUCH OUR SOULS

Poetry is what keeps many of us sane. It allows us to meet new territories within ourselves without doing too much.

NEW BEGINNINGS

There is a distance between where I am and where I want to be. It is not a road that I can travel on, fly to, or walk across. This distance that I've created started off as a minor space that didn't matter in the grand scheme of things. It was a space I was comfortable with, something that I had always expected. The small space then grew into a larger gap, one that I had little control over. And that gap began to matter; it was always in the back of my mind. How did that space get so big? What did I do to make it extend? I must've done something wrong. And now that gap has become a distance, one where I cannot see the other end.

I've been here before, standing far away from the ideal me. But I've also been at the other end of the spectrum, where I had always wanted to be, where I once was. Fulfilled, content, happy, satisfied. Standing tall, strong heart, clear mind. It's a great place. It's where I deserve to be.

The distance, though, is one I cannot control. *How do I get back there,* I ask myself. But I do not know the answer. Maybe one day, I'll wake up, and I'll be back there. As if I had walked across or flown or traveled to the ideal in my sleep. I hope it can be that easy. I hope it is soon.

Because I know the ideal is the real me. The person I was when I was young, naive and passionate. The person I'd always been.

I'll come back to myself soon enough.

YOU'RE NEVER STUCK WHERE YOU ARE

There are moments in your life when you grow instantly. Your mind and your being are changed in a split second. You feel it right away, and you can see yourself changing into a better version of yourself in the present moment.

But there are also elements of growth that happen gradually, slowly and unknowingly. You wake up one day and the way you think is slightly different. The way you respond to distress is distinct. The way you perceive yourself is filled with more light. The way you approach your day is more open. The way you feel is new. But you can't decipher when or how it happened, just that it did.

And what these two types of growth show about ourselves is that we are endlessly a work in progress. Constantly evolving, connecting with new parts of ourselves, and letting go of parts that no longer serve us.

The beauty in it is that either way, we're never stuck where we are. This life continuously allows us to be more than who we were yesterday.

THE MOON

Just like the moon, we go through phases of emptiness that transform into phases of fullness, and it is through each second that we slowly change, move, evolve, and shine differently. The magic is that we always have something to look forward to because this never-ending cycle is a reminder to ourselves—we will feel whole again.

THE FULL SPECTRUM

Good days provide fulfilling memories anchored in gratitude, bad days give awareness to suppressed feelings, lonely days offer a chance to connect with yourself, horrible days teach valuable lessons and great days produce a series of joyful moments. But no matter what type of day you're having, know that it is equipping you with exactly what you need at that point in time. So don't try to close, don't try to force yourself to only experience the highs, don't dismiss the bad days or wallow in the lonely days or dread the horrible days. Rather, open yourself fearlessly into the unknown with the belief that each day adds another page to your story and without that page, your story wouldn't be complete. Because what you learned on page eight is how you'll respond better to a similar experience on page sixty. And it is through the combination of those days that you understand the full spectrum of an abundant life. A life that is an endless process of learning, experiencing, cultivating, and growing.

REALIZATIONS

If you've handled a situation better than your old self would have, you've grown. If you've removed yourself from a toxic environment, you've prioritized yourself. If you've let go of negative beliefs and replaced them with uplifting ones, you've healed. If you've allowed yourself to be your authentic self with no shame, you've thrived. If you've attracted opportunities that align with your dream life, you've expanded.

Notice the changes you've experienced and adjust the narrative that you still have so much to achieve. Small steps still get you to your destination, so honor each one. Be present with them. And continue looking forward to taking another step, each and every day.

THE BETTER VERSION OF YOURSELF

Takes risks and doesn't care what people think. Feels deeply and isn't ashamed of it. Prioritizes their well-being by nourishing their body. Spreads love and kindness through each encounter. Balances confidence with humility. Says yes to things that feel aligned, says no to what doesn't serve them. Puts themselves in uncomfortable situations in order to grow. But above all, they always choose themselves.

CONTINUOUS SELF-GROWTH

Every day we have the decision to stay where we are or move to an unknown territory. We have the opportunity to either have our souls stay stagnant, to only meet a certain depth and not move past it, or to continuously charge them through experiences and new learnings to increase the invisible size of our souls. Choose the latter. Do something every day to expand your soul by as small as a percent. Experience new things. Travel to unknown places. Say words you haven't said before.

Because anytime you feel alive, anytime you feel joy, excitement, happiness, or freedom, you are allowing yourself to encounter a deeper part of your being—a part where you are unknowingly charging your own energy and raising its levels, allowing you to get closer to being acquainted with the purest version of you.

On

PURPOSE

ON OUR OWN TIME

Maybe our youth isn't supposed to be the time where we figure everything out, the time where we understand who we're supposed to be. Maybe all that we need to do is just move through these years—experience everything and anything—by making those mistakes, falling in and out of love, giving too much of ourselves, saying the right and wrong things, taking multiple paths, and going on several different journeys. Falling ten times, just to get up again on the eleventh. Understanding what fuels us and what makes us feel empty. Being acquainted with what brings us joy and what robs us from our happiness. Because that is how we learn, adapt, grow and transform and maybe not knowing where we're going will eventually lead us to our virtues. While we may not have much insight into where we're headed, what we want to devote our lives to or who we're supposed to be, these years are for us to experience, to be here, to feel it all, and ride the rollercoaster of life. One day, we'll end up exactly where we're destined to be, however, we get there, whenever we get there. And that is when we can look back on these years and realize why things happened the way they did.

OUR CHILDLIKE SELVES NEVER LEAVE US

Society has built this notion that life is something that we have to get through—a series of moments and experiences that pass, happen, and are forgotten about—and that one day, we'll wake up and be on the other side. As adults, we pass our time through banal routines, never-ending stress, and joyless events.

But when we think back to our childlike selves, we collectively had something special. We'd dream versus following the commonalities of others. We'd participate in activities that we selectively chose. We never thought about the past or future but instead, enjoyed where we were. We knew life was precious, but we promised ourselves that we'd never give away our power to others to dictate what life was composed of and we simply chose for ourselves.

The magic is that deep down, perhaps in a dormant state, our youthful selves are still there. Waiting to be rediscovered and brought back. That charisma, excitement, passion, grit, confidence, imagination and everything in between is ready to be reconnected with. If activated, the inner joy will be felt, and our lives can be as radiant and worthwhile as it once was.

86,400

You are given 84,600 seconds every day
Unused time is not returned, nor is it carried over
It is given as a gift
One to appreciate, take advantage of
and use to its fullest potential
Don't wait for tomorrow's 86,400 seconds
to live the life you desire
Use the moments you have now
And make each one count

THE CLOCK IS NOT TICKING

How can we expect to master the rest of our lives in 24 hours?
We are given years for a reason. Each one has a purpose, so
why would we ever rush them?

DOMINO EFFECT

Back in the day I'd read words or find photographs or admire art and think to myself *I need to create my own version of this* but then self-doubt would creep in and it would say *you're not good enough* and *it won't be as powerful* so I stopped reading books and looking at pictures and admiring artwork but I felt a part of me missing, as though my mind had stopped expanding, and so my own work quieted down and I no longer felt creative or felt like I had anything to share with the world but the lack of stimulation drained my heart so one day I chose to pick up a book and immerse myself in the creations of others and slowly I'd experience their world and rather than trying to create my own version of their work I started to feel inspired again and that's when I started writing a few lines and taking a few more photographs and it was the biggest lesson I learned: that when I engage with the world and the creations of others, all I need to do is be open to experiencing the spark—the spark that ignites something within me that leads to my own unique and beautiful creations and eventually what I articulate will be powerful enough to spark something in someone else and that is the domino effect of passionate creation so why would we ever compare ourselves again knowing that we are all an expansive combined effort and manifestation of everything we've touched between one another?

KEEP MOVING

If you missed today, there will always be tomorrow
And if tomorrow comes and nothing changes,
You still have next week
Because, despite your own stillness,
The sun will keep shining
The waves will keep crashing
The birds will continue soaring
And you will still be existing
Even when nothing feels like it's changing,
Everything around you continues to move
When you are ready,
Decide to partake in that movement

PANDORA'S BOX

I write excessively. Jotting down every degree of thought. Collecting the words I've said. Taking note of what's spiraling in my inner world. Because when I write, there is a purpose to my loud, lonely, and wild mind. It allows me to unscrew the heavy chains, step outside of myself, and land in the hearts of others.

EXTRATERRESTRIAL

There is something so unusual about human beings. Spiritual at its core. Cosmic, almost. The way we make eye contact with someone and, in that mere second, our minds register the visuals in front of us that light something in the confines of our hearts inches below. The way the sensation from our lips feels like a burst of fireworks when we make a novel rhythm with that of another, it being passed back and forth between each edge. The way an energized smile can reignite dormant emotions deep inside of us or a minuscule tear swimming down someone's cheek can shed light on one of our own unhealed wounds. The fact that we randomly decide to listen to a podcast episode of a topic we have no knowledge in, only to find out a friend of ours watched a film on the same subject days prior, allowing us to connect even deeper than before. It's as though the universe is not only existing above us, around us, or far away in a light year that we cannot mentally grasp. I believe it exists here. It is between us all, deeply enclosed by us, endlessly expanding, too. It is remarkable and leads me to wonder, what if part of the reason why they say the universe is infinite is because our capacity as human beings here is boundless?

MAGNIFYING GLASS

I was fascinated by the fact that I was equally as curious about the world around me as I was for the world within me. There is an infinite amount of rooms and compartments inside of my being. There is always something new to discover in my internal universe that I can eventually leverage to serve others.

I found peace in that.

INTENTIONAL PURPOSE

You have so much within you
Things that have yet to fully form
Thoughts that are still in their first phase of life
Feelings that you've just been acquainted with
for the first time
And for once
Do not force these things, thoughts, or feelings to be released
Do not pressure yourself towards a timeline to manifest them
into reality into a tangible form
Instead, appreciate them
Feed into them
Allow them to grow
Because one day, very soon
Everything that resides in you will be available to others
And you will finally see what this entire wait was for
Why it took this many years for you to understand
what your purpose is in this life
And one day you will look at yourself in the mirror
And smile for the life you created all on your own

THE CALLING

I can't wait to do it
To prove myself wrong
To bring the ideas in my head to real life
To bring these thoughts, and these constantly
development imaginations
Into a physical form
To start
To start and never stop
To always ask for forgiveness over permission
To be busy and restless
Over something that will eventually be a deviation
of what I hold inside
To have my name known, with a warm sentiment
To impact the lives of others, with a clear intention
To life a life full of abundance, for myself
I will be there soon
This mindset that I lost, is now back
Whatever I think about, I will do
Starting now

On

MANIFESTATION

FATE

You'll know you're surrendering when you stop caring about what your day holds and instead start opening your heart to the unknown that is meant for you. Suddenly, you'll see beautiful things come into your life out of nowhere.

BECOMING

Every once in a while, you get a glimpse of the person you could be. The type of person you visualize yourself as. The type of life you strive to have. Hold onto that. Work for it. Take the steps needed to become it. Make an effort every day to bridge the gap between your current self and your ideal self.

Nothing is out of reach.

RE-FOCUS

What you place your attention on is what will manifest in your life. We go through most of our days thinking about the negatives over the positives. We occupy most of our head with things that went wrong, words we wish we never said, or things we want to get rid of, rather than thinking about the things that went right, the sweet words we would say again or things we want in abundance.

Place your attention on what you want more of. Change the dialogue in your head. Don't think of what could've been or what was; think about what you crave to have to a greater extent. Think about what a good, happy life means to you. And every day, choose to act in a way that lets you live out the dreams your mind creates.

BRINGING YOUR IDEAL SELF INTO REALITY

Spend time every day imagining your ideal self. Picture what you'd look like, how you'd speak, and your tone towards those that can do nothing for you. Think about how you'd act in uncomfortable situations, how you'd push through difficult scenarios, or how you'd come up from being underwater. Picture what your wardrobe consists of, the environment you'd live in, and the places you'd explore. Visualize the memories you'd like to create with your closest friends and the success of the business your child self once dreamt of. Envision how you'd act, walk, think, believe, laugh, smile, move and speak. Visualize your ideal self and now, do everything in your power to become that person. Because if you were able to imagine and feel them—then they exist. But it is only up to you and your power to become it. It is only up to you to match the energy that lays dormant within you and that aligns with the world you envision living in.

A NOTE ON ENERGY

They say that energy cannot be created nor destroyed, so what if we challenged ourselves—what if we took that low energy that resides in our bodies, that flows from our minds to our limbs, those emotions that we feel in our hearts and in our souls, and transformed it into something that positively fuels us. Perhaps a thought, an awakening, a bodily movement. What if we learned to use that energy that is within us—the one we're trying so hard to get rid of, to move past, to leave behind, to ignore—and transformed it into something greater?

Only then will we understand that everything we need to live the lives we dream for is already within us. It is simply how we use the different elements that reside in our bodies and souls and transform them into the frequency that we seek.

WE ARE MEANT FOR MORE

Often we simmer too long on the negative feelings we endure—depression, anxiety, stress, unhappiness, sadness—and we tend to forget that these instances where we feel the lowest, when we feel like we're underwater with no oxygen in sight, where we think our goals cannot be achieved or that the person we hoped we would become will only exist in our minds—are actually beautiful reminders that we are meant for more. These cues show us that our current lifestyles, experiences, and mindsets are not serving or feeding our souls.

So rather than focusing on detaching from these lower feelings, we must first understand that they are there to teach us, to guide us, and to enlighten us. Only then will we realize that we are meant to live a life that is more abundant, joyful, and blissful. And it is in that moment where we can choose to change our realities.

LIVING THE LIFE YOU'VE ALWAYS IMAGINED

There will be moments in your current chapter where you feel like the life you desire to live feels out of touch and out of sight. That all the reveries in your mind will stay stagnant there, never fully manifesting into where your feet are. Those moments will be puzzling—you'll feel like you've gone backward in your life trajectory that you've always imagined and that you're far from experiencing all that you want to take in from this life.

But then there will be a moment where you get a glimpse of the life you've always desired—you'll have a taste of the lifestyle you know you were destined to have, the people you want to be surrounded by, and the happiness you know you've been yearning to feel. In that moment, hold onto it. Cherish it. Take note of it. Write down the experience by describing the sensations and feelings associated with it.

Because soon after, you'll have another moment. And then a third. And then a fourth, and so on. And you will think back to the very first, remembering where and how this all started. Those moments will show how the life you pictured yourself having no longer just holds a place in your mind—it'll be the life you start to live, sustaining the joys associated with each.

That life is worth sticking around for.

UNLOCKING YOUR POTENTIAL

The better version of yourself that lives in your mind—the person who speaks with poise, walks with confidence, and travels with liberation, or the person whose career is successful, whose relationships are healthy, and whose health is flourishing—is no different than the you right now. The person you want to be is the same person who is breathing in and out, who's taking steps, who's partaking in life right at this moment. The only differences between you and them are their mindsets, their habits, and their beliefs. It's the way they think, their daily practices, and the words they tell themselves.

How liberating is that? That the person you want to be isn't that far off, and becoming them isn't some intimating threshold that feels far out of reach. Instead, that person is accessible to you and at any moment, you can choose to welcome them. By shifting your mindset and embodying that person, you can unlock their being—and you can become the better you now.

FROM THE MIND TO THE REALITY

The common misconception about manifestation is that if only we visualize where we want to be, the universe will listen and provide what it is we are seeking. But the work doesn't end with us simply visualizing the end destination—that's just the start.

The real transformations in our lives occur when we visualize the steps we must take in order to get there. It's imagining the person you want to become, feeling their existence, embodying how they carry themselves, how they speak, how they walk, how they act. It's imagining the necessary steps needing to be taken—understanding what you need to let go of, what you need to act on, what micro goals you must accomplish, what decisions you must take in the present moment. And although we must trust the universe to deliver on the how, the combined process of setting clear intentions, acting, believing, and envisioning is when our manifestations will become our realities.

WHAT IF

It all worked out? The visions in your mind are brought to reality in a way better than you've imagined? The goals you've been working hard to reach are met? The desire to be acquainted with your ideal partner is fulfilled? Your inner trauma is finally healed and released?

Open your heart to the possibility that it all can work out. Feel what you'd feel if everything you dreamed of was already a part of your life. Place yourself in environments where you can experience all that you imagine yourself experiencing. Because when you match the vibration of the universe, it will slowly place you in front of new doors, give you the strength to open them and allow you to reach whatever it is you're seeking.

EVERYTHING IS WITHIN YOUR REACH

Everything you are searching to bring into your world is accessible to you. But what we often miss is the fact that receiving starts with simply believing that you can access it. Whenever you daydream about the things you want to bring into your life, it can either be from a place of excitement and faith or from a place of fear and uncertainty. The former is what you should strive to feel throughout your journey, as it means you already have confidence that you have the power to achieve it and that it already belongs to you. But believing isn't enough—you need to act in accordance with that vibration. You have to take risks. You have to get back up, even when you fall. You have to ignore what others think. You have to remove anything that hinders your peace and make space for what fuels your soul. You have to put yourself first. You have to be 100% you. When you are internally aligned, your reality will match. Everything you are manifesting will be brought into your life, and at that moment, you will be ready to receive it.

HOLDING HANDS WITH THE UNIVERSE

When you ask the universe for love, it'll send you experiences where people show their value to you, and it'll remove anyone who doesn't measure the sensation you are seeking. When you ask for patience, the universe will present opportunities where you are forced to combat restlessness and discontent. When you ask the universe to help you heal, it'll throw you into a storm where the disturbance shakes you up and makes you rethink your thought patterns. When you ask for something better, the universe will remove what no longer aligns with your grand vision. When you're falling, the universe will whisper the sweet words, *"Trust me, it's happening for a reason."* When you're soaring high, the universe will affirm its position by saying, *"See, I told you so!"*

The universe is your partner. It is your guide. It is the home you find comfort in, the bed you can fall back on, the portal for your dreams. Your role in this relationship is to surrender, to act with compliance, to change your perspective, and to appreciate all of the lessons that will soon come to fruition. It's not just you, it's not just the universe—it's the alliance you share that creates the life you aspire to experience.

UNCOVERING YOURSELF, AGAIN

There are periodic moments in your life where you feel far from the person you know you are at your core. You feel misaligned and imbalanced. Confusion, desperation, nostalgia, pain and loneliness all orbit around your heart and your mind. Your past self is missed, your future self is out of sight and your current self is numb. But these periodic moments are hidden blessings that validate how lucky you are. To feel things so intensely. To be able to listen to your mind and body and hear what they are telling you. To be able to witness when you are not in equilibrium. And so the next time you find yourself looking in the mirror and seeing an unrecognizable figure, remind yourself that it's all temporary. That what you're feeling today doesn't have to linger, but it does have a deeper purpose—to bring you closer to the path that is right. Soon, you will be yourself again (but if you're lucky, which you are), you will have more knowledge than before, and those moments are what help you evolve into a better version of your previous self.

THIS MESSAGE IS FOR YOU

No matter how painful it feels, no matter how lost your soul is, no matter how lonely your heart is, there is something greater out there for you. So what if I told you that six months from now, you'd be living your dream life? That you'd have the relationship you're seeking, or the job that fuels you, or the good health you've been searching for. But instead of continuously wishing for the future (where everything feels pleasant), be where your feet are and bring it into existence in the now.

Today might be the day when the universe answers all of your prayers. Today might be the day that you meet someone who changes your life. Today might be the day you surprise yourself with all of your glory. And the only way to experience these changes is by opening your mind, breaking down your closed-off walls, and inviting in what the world has brought to you. There is always room for new beginnings and an evolution of your being. You just have to be open to experiencing them.

JEREMIAH 29:11

Every once in a while, you will hear a little voice inside of you that says, *"Here. Here it is. This is what I was praying for."* And you will feel an overwhelming amount of warmth knowing that your higher power is always listening and making all things work beautifully together for your virtue. He never misses anything. He never gives up on you. He never leaves you. Even when the waters are calm, whisper your gratitude. When the tides are rough, speak your desires. When the waves crash, surrender your control.

One day, you will have everything you've ever prayed for. But in the meantime, continue to build your trust, carry your hope, and maintain your faith. That is how the little voice inside of you will continue to notice all of the blessings.

A REASON TO KEEP GOING

Even if the current circumstances in your life make you question how you'll ever get to where you want to be, you have to understand that everything you are currently experiencing or have experienced has a purpose. Because those previous steps brought you to where you are today, molding you into the person that you are. But remember: there are still so many moments to experience that will bring you joy and closer to your destiny. More laughs, more books to read, more people to meet, more risks, more love, more pictures to take, more songs to discover, more places to see, and more food to taste. Once you believe you're worthy of experiencing more, you'll realize you have the power within you to bring those things to life, and you'll see the world differently.

WILLING HANDS

Even if a little voice inside of you whispers, *"you can't do this,"* your willing hands must respond back and say, *"watch me."* If your dreams don't terrify you at least a little bit, then what's the point of dreaming?

432 HZ

I closed my eyes and found a world waiting to be explored
I opened my eyes and realized I can create that world

LIMITLESS

She knew the power of her mind
So she used it wisely
Constantly dreaming
Visualizing
Thinking
Dismissing any self-doubt
Removing all hindrances
Detaching from what didn't serve her
Trusting what her heart whispered
To the point where the visuals in her mind
And the experiences in her reality
Became one and the same

THE MAESTRO

She knew she evolved when her success
no longer surprised her
Because somewhere deep within her
She trusted that she could do it all

On

LIFE

THE THINGS THEY DON'T TEACH YOU

As I grow older and am exposed to a larger world, or am acquainted with all sorts of people—from ethnicity to class, from happy individuals to lonely ones—I have learned that it is not the jewelry on your neck nor the size of your home nor the price tag of your car. It is the people around you, the love that you give and feel, and the smiles you encounter from those closest to you that will bring pure joy into your life. Because once all of that stuff is taken away and you are stranded alone, where will you find happiness? After all, the feeling we all strive for, what we are told has the highest value in life, is felt the deepest when it is caused by the people that you love and who love you back. So rather than spending on an item that provides momentary excitement, spend your time, the most precious asset we all have, with those you love. Engage with them. Experience life with them. Explore them. Make memories with them. It is through those moments you participate in that you will allow yourself to achieve pure joy and happiness in this short life.

WHAT IT'S REALLY ABOUT

The best thing you can do for yourself is to actually do the things that fuel you. I'm not talking about getting a job that just pays the bills, or making plans with 'friends' just so your Saturday night isn't spent alone, or going on a three-mile run because you ate more than usual last night. I'm talking about finding your passion and making it your work. I'm talking about building healthy relationships with individuals who expand your mind and make you feel safe. I'm talking about finding a form of movement that makes you feel strong and is a form of release. I'm talking about finding a partner that loves you wholly and satisfies your desires. I'm talking about spending every breathing moment doing things that bring you joy. That brings you peace. That makes you better. Because when you move through the motions, have a routine that is unsatisfying, or spend your time with people that bring you down, you're doing a disservice to your younger self. They wanted a beautiful life for you. They imagined and dreamed and hoped. If they were standing in front of you now, would you want to tell them, *"I'm sorry I let you down"* or *"I did it—I'm living your dream life."*

FACE VALUE

Sometimes, you have to remind yourself that some things are momentary. That you are presented with situations simply to learn from them and nothing more. You want certain relationships to last, feelings to stay forever, thoughts to live by, yet when something is taken from you or when a part of you is lost, you have to look beyond what is gone and understand what you have gained. A new lesson. A realization. A fresh mindset. Because you can learn a lot from a little, and it is that new knowledge that allows you to grow into a better version of yourself and to understand what type of future you want to have. While the heartache, confusion, and the emptiness may linger, this new beginning will set you free. And the previous moments were just another step along the longer path to being who you were destined to be.

SOUL CHARGING VS. SOUL SEARCHING

Searching for your soul implies that it is not within you already, that you have to go out and find your intrinsic self. But as humans who are made up of energy, we are born with a soul that is never lost, thus, can never be searched for or found.

Sometimes that energy within you is at full capacity—you feel joyful, happy, content, fulfilled, satisfied. But at other stages of your life, the energy you feel is less than full capacity, a quarter of what you know your soul has the potential to be. All you must do is change the dialogue. Don't search for what is already within you. Rather, immerse yourself in experiences that will naturally charge your soul.

LABYRINTH OF MEMORIES

Why is it that I constantly feel the need to classify every oc-
currence that I experience in my mind? It's as though I have
a library living within me; folders and shelves and novels all
organized by similar and novel feelings, emotions and events,
a collection of classics and bestsellers and new releases, all by
the same author that is me. A private space that I often revisit;
as if I'm unable to simply move through life without trying
to fully understand, analyze and uncover what each moment
holds. I have this recurring fixation on trying to establish
where each new experience fits within my collection; attempt-
ing to arrange it accurately, truthfully, and without error.

But sometimes I wish I could stop needing to fully unravel the
meaning each moment holds, before I allow myself to move
past it. Sometimes I wish I could stop trying to comprehend
how the present moment is connected to a similar experience
from years prior. Sometimes I wish I could just live and not
think about how I'm living.

But then again, this is the intimate part of myself that holds all of the joyful memories, moments of growth, deep realizations, peaks of enlightenment, bursts of light, stages of darkness and spectrum of emotions I've felt throughout my lifetime. And so maybe taking note of every occurrence is a good thing, because it is an accumulation and collection of all that I have experienced, and will soon experience, in my time here on earth.

I'm starting to believe that the history of my existence is worth building a library for, as it's where my greatest lessons, truths and wisdom lie. One day when I'm older I'll open the door again with nothing but a smile on my face and peace in my heart, knowing it all existed. Knowing that *I* existed.

LESS EXPECTATIONS, MORE JOY

When you reflect on your past and think about the best moments in your life, ask yourself, what about this moment was so great? Was it who I was surrounded by? Was it the location I was in? Was it because I felt so confident in my skin? Or maybe it isn't something you can generalize since each of those moments were unique and different from one another that it is impossible to pinpoint the common denominator that made each of those experiences so wonderful.

Perhaps, then, the best moments in our lives aren't about the external factors around us, but instead about our mindset at that point in time. Maybe it was that the internal dialogue in our minds had no expectations, allowing ourselves to fully surrender to the universe with open energy and a positive mindset, not thinking about what should or could be. Sometimes we set our expectations too low, limiting our potential or the experiences' possibilities. Other times, we set unrealistic or unattainable expectations, causing a lot of frustration, heartbreak, and unhappiness.

As you move through life, live without expectations. Place yourself in quality circumstances, surround yourself with people you love, and be open to what the world has to offer. This is how you expose yourself to even more pure, bright moments and increase the number of wholesome memories.

GIVE YOURSELF PERMISSION

Every day we make countless decisions and partake in many actions, but what we often forget to do in this life is to just let ourselves be. We forget to give ourselves permission to feel joy, to be happier, to have memorable moments, to laugh more, to feel deeper, to take that solo trip, to say those words we've been hiding internally. We create confines in ourselves for no reason that prevent us from living a fulfilling, radiant life. Or we find ways to self-sabotage from living the life we truly crave and deserve.

Allow yourself to be a better you, to experience new patterns, to have challenging thoughts, to think in different ways, to feel deeper emotions. Grant yourself permission to say no, to choose yourself over others, to taste new dishes, or immerse yourself in new cultures.

It's not about whether we're capable or whether we have the resources; it's about whether we permit ourselves to live through this adventure.

SIX QUESTIONS TO ASK YOURSELF DAILY

Does this align with the life I want to live?
Is this person/thing raising my energy, or lowering it?
Does this serve my greater purpose?
Are my actions in tune with the better version of myself?
Does this make me feel good now,
and will it make me feel good later?
Are the choices I am making solely for myself, or for others?

LETTING LIFE BE

There are moments in our lives where they aren't as beautiful as we once hoped. Our hearts will break, people will tear us down, we'll witness changes that we weren't mentally prepared for. We will lose friends we thought we'd grow old with or lovers who we imagined would be by our side until the end. We'll experience loss, confusion, stress, and worry, leading us to question, *is this really it?*

But there are moments when our energy is radiating, where everything falls into place. Lovers give us what we desire, we laugh with our true friends until our stomachs ache, we're able to travel to places we thought only existed in photographs taken by others and we experience occurrences where every emotion and sensation is heightened, feeding our souls. Moments where those negative thoughts only hold a minimal space in the back of our minds, allowing us to be present and savor the various thrills of life.

We must be grateful for all of it.

LIVING IN HARMONY

Simply put, all you need to aim for in this life is balance. Be fearless, but don't forget to slow down and enjoy the now. Be content with all you have, but never stop improving yourself. Be kindhearted, but don't let others mistreat you. Be independent, but rely on others when you need support. Give your trust, but not to those who are deceiving. Be shamelessly selfish, but learn to also be altruistic. Because a balanced life isn't a perfect or fragile one, but instead, it's one that is harmonious—giving us the space, time, energy, and freedom for what truly matters.

FORMULA

Dream, and then act
Start, and then continue
Fall, but then get up
Learn, and move on
Repeat,
Again
And again

This is how you live and grow

AN EXHAUSTIVE LIST OF THINGS
TO DO MORE OF

Be sillier

Cry it out

Act your age

Book that trip

Try new things

Get a massage

Open your heart

Relax, loosen up

Break more walls

Go to that concert

Say hi to strangers

Eat what you crave

Take more chances

Say yes and always go

Make more mistakes

Pick up some flowers

Dance in your room alone

Scream when you need to

Tell them those three words

Be unapologetically yourself

Let your childlike spirit come out

Buy that thing you can't get your mind off of

Live each day like it's your last 24 hours on this earth

HUMAN EXPERIENCE

The purpose of life is not to feel bliss at every moment, it is to find equilibrium through the entire spectrum of emotions. We must allow ourselves to witness every dimension our feelings can go, to experience all that our minds and hearts are capable of. Remove the self-inflicted pressure to be happy and joyful all of the time. Get rid of the idea that you are failing anytime you feel sad, empty, or angry. All you need to do is strive to be in a place where you are no longer judging yourself for what you are naturally feeling. You must invite in every emotion, thought, and feeling that arises as they come. That is how you'll live a raw, dimensional, and authentic human experience.

EVERYTHING HAPPENS AS IT SHOULD

Every moment, decision, choice, encounter, person, mistake, lesson, step forwards, step backwards, heartbreak, love, failure, breakthrough, dream…are the little dots that create the sum of your entire life. Each experience leads to the next and although in the present moment it may seem that everything is scattered all over the place, one day you will be able to connect the dots between each part of your life. When you do, you will have the realization that a life void of even just one of those dots, would not have made you the person that you are. Trust that everything happens as it should, in a way that is right for you. Maintain that faith and you will experience the freedom you are seeking.

SWING SET

In order to level up your life, you need to expose yourself to new levels. Immerse yourself in experiences that make you feel uncomfortable. Befriend individuals who are further along than you. Date someone who's out of your league. Start your dream business you have no credentials in. Go exploring, go running, go persisting. The discomfort is what will take you to a new playing field. One that your inner child has been yearning to play in.

HYPERAWARENESS

I look at the people around me with disbelief
That they can experience life without constantly thinking
about the meaning behind the occurrences they face
How they can face adversity and not wonder, *why me?*
How they can fall in and out of love and not question what
childhood trauma may still linger
How they can have their dreams fall apart
yet not reflect on how they got to that point
I was fascinated by how others lived without being aware
of their thoughts, without yearning to dig deeper
I always wondered what that would be like
But then I discovered
This is my superpower
I am better off this way

TRADE OFF

Everything in life is an energetic exchange
What you pour into, will flow back towards you
Select wisely

BEYOND THE VISIBLE
OBSERVABLE UNIVERSE

The magic doesn't happen when you sit in your misery. Wild experiences don't occur when you play it safe. Blissful moments don't occur when you spend time with people who drain you. The only way you will feel alive is when you step outside of your comfort zone. It is when your heart sends you a signal, and you lean into it. Those are the moments that feel supernatural.

AUTHENTICITY

This life is not about finding yourself, for that implies that your being is elsewhere—apart from you, with others, buried somewhere deep, living presently in a different dimension. This life is about uncovering yourself by peeling off the layers that society has built upon you, for that implies that who you are at your core is with you at all times—your beliefs, character, personality, purpose, aspirations. It simply has yet to be recollected.

Do not try to find yourself, for you will spend an eternity chasing something that can never be found. Instead, look inwards and you will find that everything you have been seeking has been with you all along. It just needs to be remembered.

HUMAN EXPERIMENT

We all take this life for granted. We are all part of a fascinating scientific experiment—being a human being is extraordinarily bewildering but nevertheless, it is a mesmerizing experience to be part of. We think, we feel, we learn, we innovate, we move, we digest, we hear, we listen, we touch, we create, we pivot, we fail, we succeed, we laugh, we cry, we move mountains, we tear down cultures, we say I love you followed by I can't do this anymore, we breathe, we close, we hurt, we heal, and in the blink of a moment, we go from everything to nothing and nothing to everything. But what is purely fascinating is that we are evolving every day collectively, together, and independently, quickly and slowly, and although what tomorrow holds will forever be a mystery, we are all here together, at this time, creating our futures, creating *the* future.

If we can't be anything, we should at least try to be grateful because when will we ever get to do this again? When will we ever get to simultaneously be part of the greatest scientific experiment where no placebo has been given, where results are ambiguous, where a conclusion can never be made?

We must find it within ourselves to appreciate it all—because this moment, right here, will one day be history. And we should make every second count.

A COLLABORATIVE EXISTENCE

All of us are an accumulation of each and every soul that we have all collectively touched. Our thoughts derive from someone else's wisdom, our energy an imitation, our desires as citations, our mindset a byproduct of the experiences of others. A part of us will always exist elsewhere, with or without our knowledge, and our individual existence is an accumulation of all that has influenced us. And it's quite beautiful. Knowing that our souls, habits, mannerisms, expressions, words, movements and everything in between are connected and will forever live on—even when we are no longer with it.

TAKE US TO THE PLACE

When you finally believe that life's greatest joys are worth waiting for, you'll wait differently.

SCHOLAR

Become a student of life
Study all that is around you
Take note of every experience
Write pages of what your feelings hold
Cross off things you want to do
Highlight memories you yearn to keep
Immerse yourself in new topics
Digest the intricacies of the people around you
Befriend the professor that is the universe
Be devoted
Through time and attention
To continuously acquire knowledge
From what exists beyond your physical body
And trust that there will always be something novel out there
That will bring you closer to home

MANIFESTO FOR LIVING

Dream on and dream big, but don't worry how it'll happen. Daily progress will get you there. Open your heart, but don't think too much about when you'll meet your person. Your patience will be worthwhile. Nourish your body, but don't put a time constraint on when you need to look and feel your best. Your body will transform once you remove the pressure. Splurge on experiences, but try not to stress about your finances. When you invest in yourself, money will always flow back. Plan your future, but don't forget to enjoy where you are. The present moment and our accomplishments are gifts we often take advantage of. Put your intentions out there, but detach from the outcome. It's preventing you from manifesting your desires. Embark on grand adventures, but also participate in the little spontaneous moments in your daily life. They are the source of your biggest joys and fulfillment. Release and let go, but don't forget to acknowledge the lessons learned. Your past made you who you are today. Find a creative outlet, but don't pressure yourself toward perfection. Your inner child just wants to play. Embrace your vulnerability, but don't overthink. Your emotional bravery will allow you to deepen your connections with others. Once you find the balance between it all, you will stumble upon serenity.

CHANGE YOUR STORY

When you take a bird's-eye view of your life, how does it make you feel? Are you proud of the decisions you've made? Are you content with your surroundings? Do you feel bliss during your daily routine? Are your experiences fulfilling you? Do you feel passion for your work? Is the relationship you have with yourself filled with love?

If you are not satisfied with your life—if you are misaligned with the way you have been living—then go out into the world and change it. Allow yourself to shift what you see from a bird's eye view. Set clear intentions on the life you do want to live and how you want to feel. Make decisions from the perspective of who you want to become, and start acting in accordance with that version of you. You owe it to yourself to design a life worth feeling pride for.

GET EXCITED ABOUT LIFE

If there are bridges you have yet to walk across, mountains you have yet to look up to, airports you have yet to touch base in, souls you have yet to encounter, oceans you have yet to be enveloped in, flowers you have yet to pick, songs you have yet to hear...then why would you ever think that what you have already experienced is all there is? Eight billion people in this world, intend to meet more of them. Seven wonders of this world, set out to reach them. Conversations in your mind, plan on speaking them. Be satisfied and grateful for what you have, but feel excitement for what else exists that you have yet to make contact with. This life is meant to be experienced to its fullest potential, and once you believe that, you'll build faith within you that one day, you will be across that potential. Hand to hand. Face to face. Heart to heart.

ENJOY THE RIDE

There are many places I have yet to see, feelings I have yet to encounter, experiences I have yet to fulfill, people I have yet to cross paths with, wisdom I have yet to learn, and dreams that have not been brought into reality and so when people ask me, *"What is your biggest fear?"* My only response is, *"There is so much my soul craves to experience in this lifetime, and I am scared that I won't get to witness all of it."*

But at the same time, I have done so much, I have learned so much, I have seen so much, I have felt so much, I have healed so much, I have traveled so much, I have tried so much and I have grown so much. But is there a minimum? Is there a limit? How far can I go?

All I can do is continue—and see where the experiences of my lifetime take me.

AFTERWORD

To share an intimate and vulnerable part of me with the world feels like a long-lasting hug—I at first didn't want to let go, it felt safe to hold onto these words. But I knew that handing off my energy, thoughts, and wisdom will linger longer than myself, and that I must pass off my learnings with others so they can feel a new level of love and warmth. Thank you for being here and for supporting me.

I started writing this book on February 2nd, 2013, when I was only sixteen years old. Unknowingly, though. This book is a time capsule—from words that my hopeless 16-year-old self wrote, to the heaviness that my chaotic 20-year-old self felt, to the liberation that my current self-assured 25-year-old self is experiencing. Every word in this novel is a testament to all of the fear, heartbreak, confusion, and loneliness I once endured, that all intricately allowed me to unravel deeper parts of myself. As a result, those moments gave me the ability to live more presently, embody self-love, heal, grow, evolve, and ultimately feel an overwhelming amount of freedom and gratitude. In every chapter, you will notice the shifts that I have experienced throughout my lifetime, proving that it is possible to change your mindset and your life.

Beauty in the Stillness first started as a way for me to release all that was built up inside of my heart and mind. I never imagined that I'd ever publish my work (although at 16-years-old I did write it as a line item on my bucket list), but as I continued to experience the various highs and lows of life, I would often write scribbles or jot down random thoughts whenever I was in need of clarity, fuel, inspiration or strength. They eventually evolved into poems and essays, and it wasn't until I decided to share my work online with the world that I realized—we are all more alike than I ever thought and there is a strong effect when you share yourself with the world.

Over the years, I learned that in order to develop a healthy relationship with myself—a relationship filled with self-love and gratitude—I needed to first understand myself. Understand who I am, who I am not, why I think the way I think, why I see the things I see, why I feel the things I feel. It's the cycle of learning and unlearning that I've committed to and will continue to commit to, as the benefits I've reaped have been extraordinary. Not only has it allowed me to discover myself and shed layers that no longer align with the path I'm on, but it also has allowed me to serve you all, so you can too.

Anytime I am able to articulate the inner feelings and deep emotions—through a combination of 26 different letters that somehow form comprehensible sentences in which depict exactly what I'm enduring within—I feel a sense of freedom. Lightness. Liberation. It is through the power of words—the power of removing attachments to certain thoughts, feelings, or emotions, isolating my understanding of a situation, articulating it, and just being there with it—that I noticed myself truly growing. Because this process offers me clarity, enabling me to see beyond my circumstances and move past them into a newer version of myself. This is how I have become compassionate for my entire disposition. This is how I have become my authentic self.

The biggest lesson I've learned over the past few years is this—everything I have ever experienced in my life, or will experience, is meant for me. It is happening *for* me. And so I must appreciate it all. Everything is temporary, the highs and the lows, but that is the adventure of this lifetime. If it weren't for those painful, debilitating, numb moments in my past, I wouldn't feel the joy, bliss, gratitude, or freedom I am now experiencing, at the extent I'm experiencing them in. I am who I am because of it all, and I wouldn't want it any other way (and neither should you). And now, I no longer feel worried if things don't go as planned or when my heart feels heavier, or if I feel stuck. I create space for it, I honor it, I learn from it. This is how I've allowed myself to truly surrender to whatever life brings to me—the negative and the positive. This is what I call living a truthful, human existence.

I hope you found yourself in these words. I hope a part of you leaves feeling lighter, clearer and happier. I hope these entries give you the strength to keep going, and I hope you come back to these words when you feel like you can't. I hope my story allows you to see that dreams can come true, that you can heal, that you can love yourself wholly. I hope you feel inspired to unbecome what no longer resonates and become whoever it is you want to become.

I am grateful that you are here. I hope you are too.

ACKNOWLEDGEMENTS

I genuinely cannot describe the level of gratitude I feel. This book is a testament to every human being I have ever crossed paths with, whether my relationship with them is a long-lasting one or simply someone who quickly passed by, like a distinct bird that rests on your windowsill, beautiful and mesmerizing, that you likely will never see again. Every person I have ever forged a connection with is the reason why I have been able to write this book. They left some sort of mark on me that opened new doors internally, ultimately allowing me to connect deeper with myself.

A few heartfelt and special '*thank yous*' I must express...

Mom and dad—from day one, you have shown me what unconditional love is. You both have been my biggest supporters, my strongest friends, my guiding lights, and the home I can always come back to. You know me better than anyone else, sometimes better than I know myself, and the fact that I have two selfless souls who I can share my darkest thoughts with or the greatest joys is something I have grown to truly appreciate. You have held me at my lowest and cheered me on at my highest, and I wouldn't be who I am today without the two of you, literally and figuratively. Over the years, as I have become my authentic self, I have noticed that all of the parts of me that I love the most are derived from you two. Thank you, thank you, thank you. The love I have for you two is immeasurable, but I trust that it is endless.

Alek—we are so different yet so alike in many ways. Ever since our youth, you have been the person I have looked up to the most. As we've both grown up, you have shown me what it means to be authentically yourself. You walk on your own path and disregard what doesn't feel in alignment. You say you'll do something and you do it. You create a dream and you bring it to life. You know your worth and you never settle for anything less. You may not know it, but you have inspired me in more ways than you'd ever believe. Thank you for paving the way and for showing me what it means to be a passionate, driven and kind soul. Sometimes I wonder what I did to deserve you being my brother. Then again, I'm also a great sister, so I guess it balances out.

Yaya—you were an angel here on earth and you are now an angel in heaven. This book wouldn't have come to fruition without your powers. As I wrote this, I'd periodically ask for a sign from above (specifically from you) that this was my destiny and that this is the path I must embark on. And, well, here we are. You experienced a lot of pain in your life but you never failed to see the light, even in the darkest of times. You showed me what strength is. You trained me into thinking more optimistically. You taught me that the greatest joys in life are brought during simple moments with those that you love. Your smile is still all that I see when I think of you, but after writing this, I have felt your presence more frequently, and now, I am smiling more than I ever have. I know you are proud of me and that you are cheering me on from above. Thank you for all that you have given me, and continue to give me, despite not physically being here.

Noelle—you believed in me and my work before I even sent you my manuscript. To me, that is a testament to how passionate and dedicated you were in allowing me to live out my dream. I thank you for not only giving me the space and opportunity to shine, but also for the creative freedom to do so in a way that felt the most right for me. You took on this book with the utmost love, devotion, and care. I can never thank you enough.

Caroline—you were the first soul I ever shared my poetry with back in 2018. I will never forget the moment where we were laying on my bed, peeling off layers of ourselves, wondering where it all went wrong and asking when the pain we were both simultaneously feeling would dissipate. It was the first time I didn't feel alone in my numbness. Thank you for believing in me and encouraging me to put myself out there. You allowed me to believe in myself, and I will forever cherish that moment. The bond we share is unlike any other and I am eternally grateful that God brought you into my life. Keep shining, Care. You are more special than you give yourself credit for.

Jack—you are the pure embodiment of, *"you never know when you'll meet someone who will change your life."* I knew we'd have a great relationship from day one on the job at Anomaly, but I never thought in a million years that my manager would also be my mentor and a dear friend. I've learned so much from you—both in business and in life—and you continuously inspire me every day to live an extraordinary, rich, abundant life rooted in my own truth. Thank you for giving me the opportunity to go after my dreams in between all the craziness we both experience at work together. If it weren't for your encouragement and the freedom you've given me, I probably wouldn't be here today. Or I might've been, but probably with more stress, less wisdom, and fewer memorable experiences.

To all of my friends, family and ICI ET NU community, I have this overwhelming feeling inside of me that cannot be explained. To experience this level of love, support, and encouragement over the years is something I never thought was attainable. I feel blessed for all of you.

Thank you.
Thank you.
Thank you.

I love you all.
Today, yesterday, always, and forever.

Xx
Karin

ABOUT THE AUTHOR

Karin is an author and founder of ICI ET NU (translated from both French and Danish, which means 'Here and Now'), a lifestyle brand that promotes living in the present moment. She's a first-generation Armenian and Assyrian soul residing in New Jersey.

instagram.com/karinhadadan
instagram.com/icietnu

MORE FROM
THOUGHT CATALOG BOOKS

A Gentle Reminder
—*Bianca Sparacino*

When You're Ready, This Is How You Heal
—*Brianna Wiest*

You Will Feel Whole Again
—*Parm K.C.*

Holding Space for the Sun
—*Jamal Cadoura*

All That You Deserve
—*Jacqueline Whitney*

All The Right Pieces
—*Nakeia Homer*